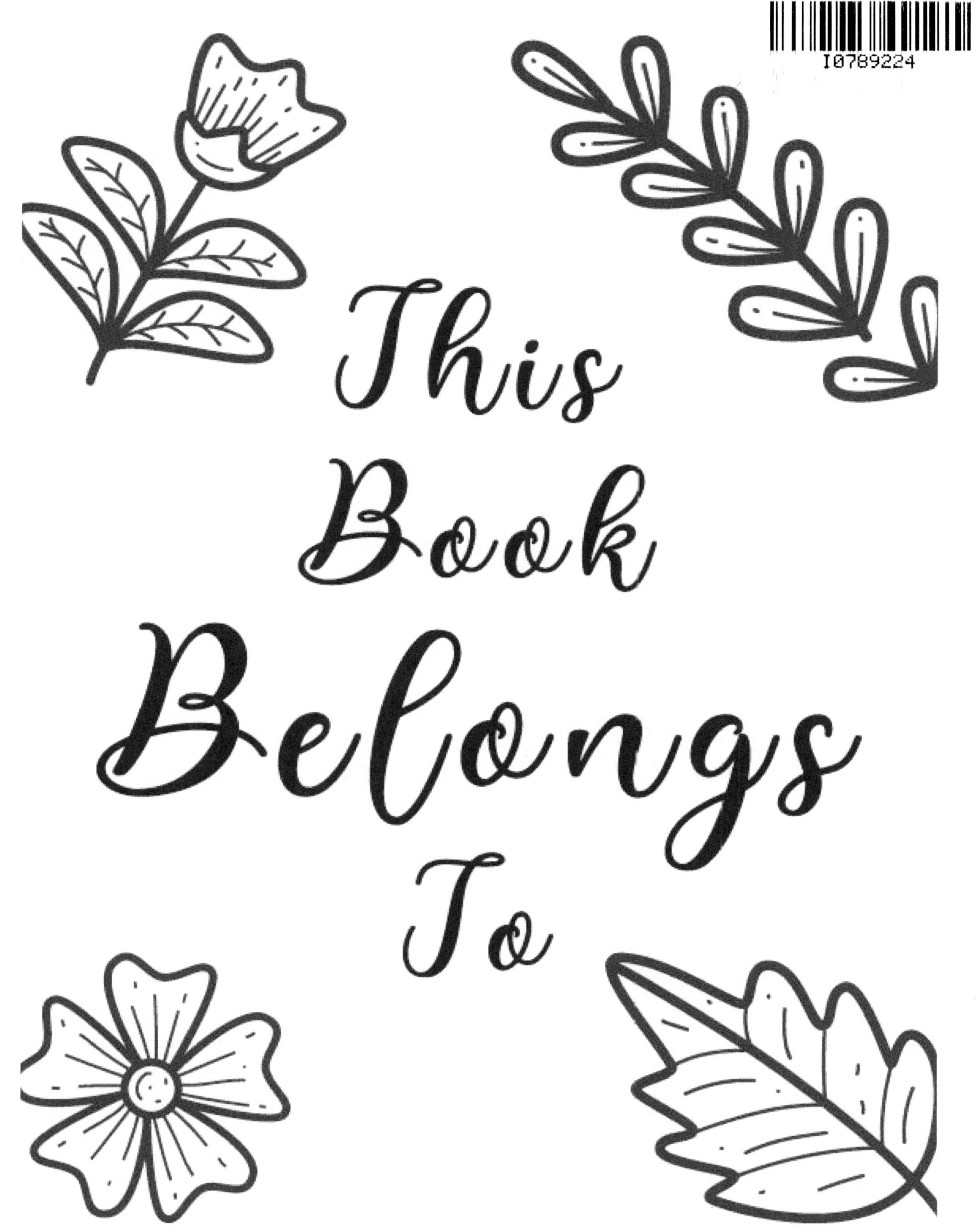

This
Book
Belongs
To

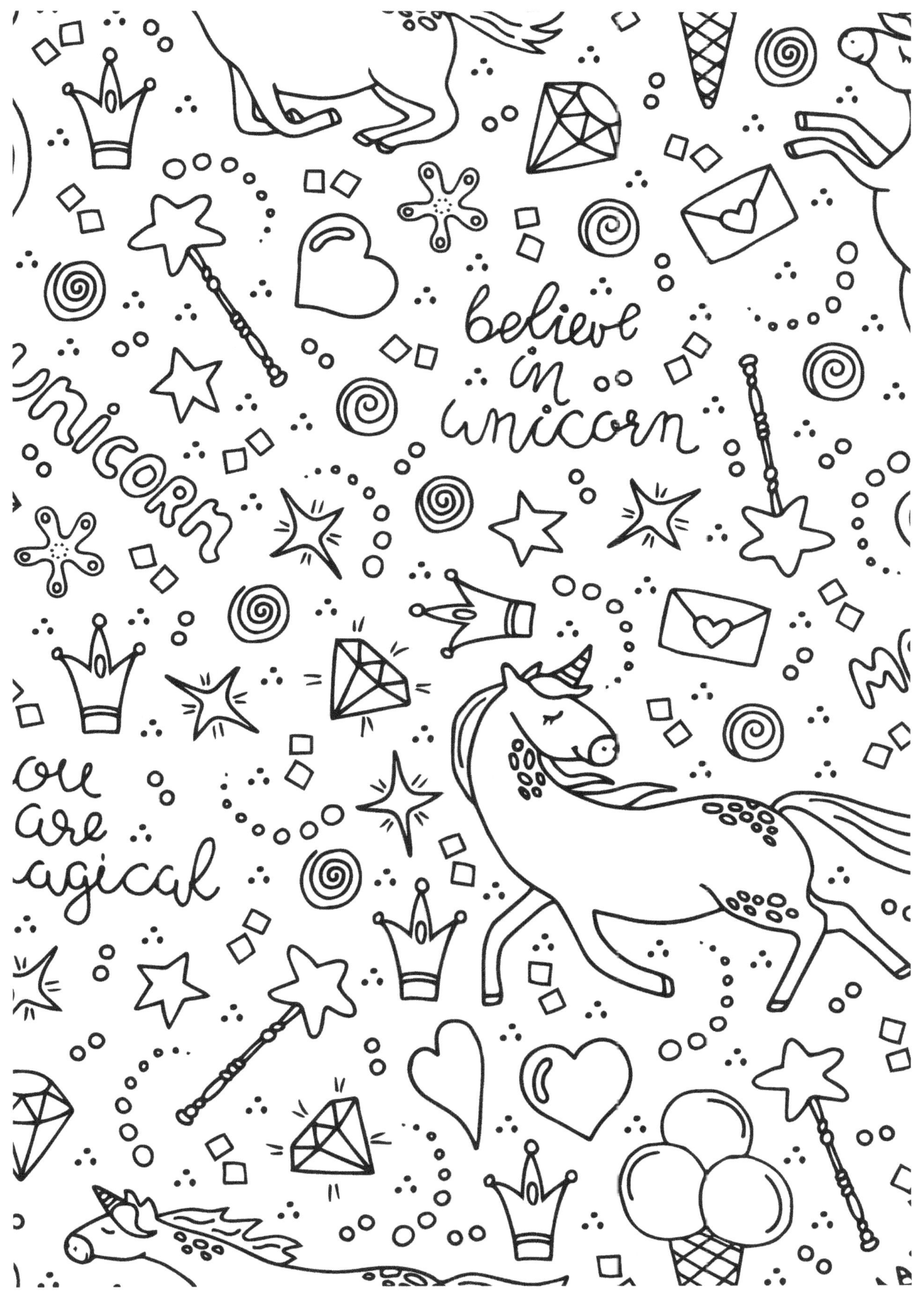

believe in unicorn
unicorn
you are magical

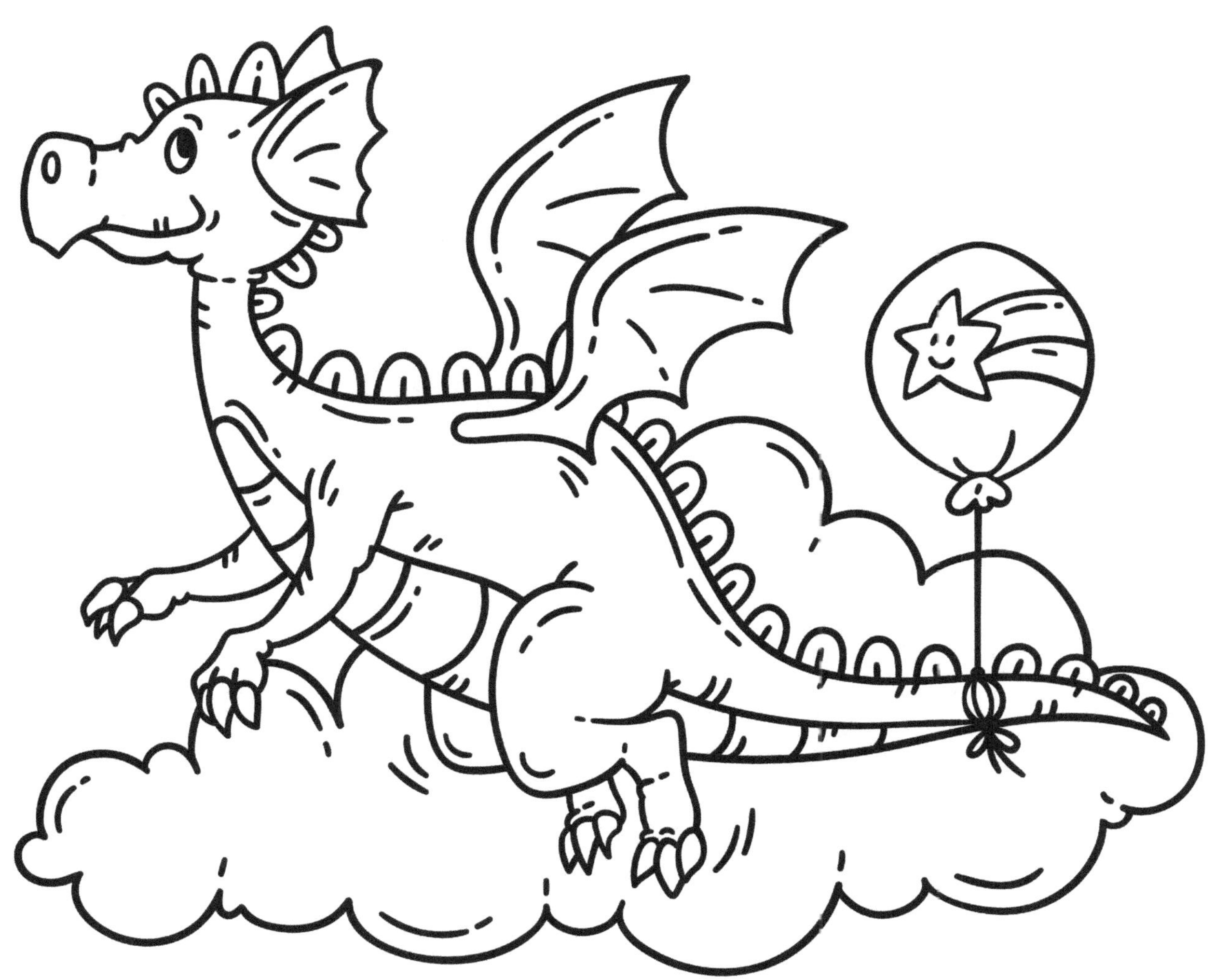

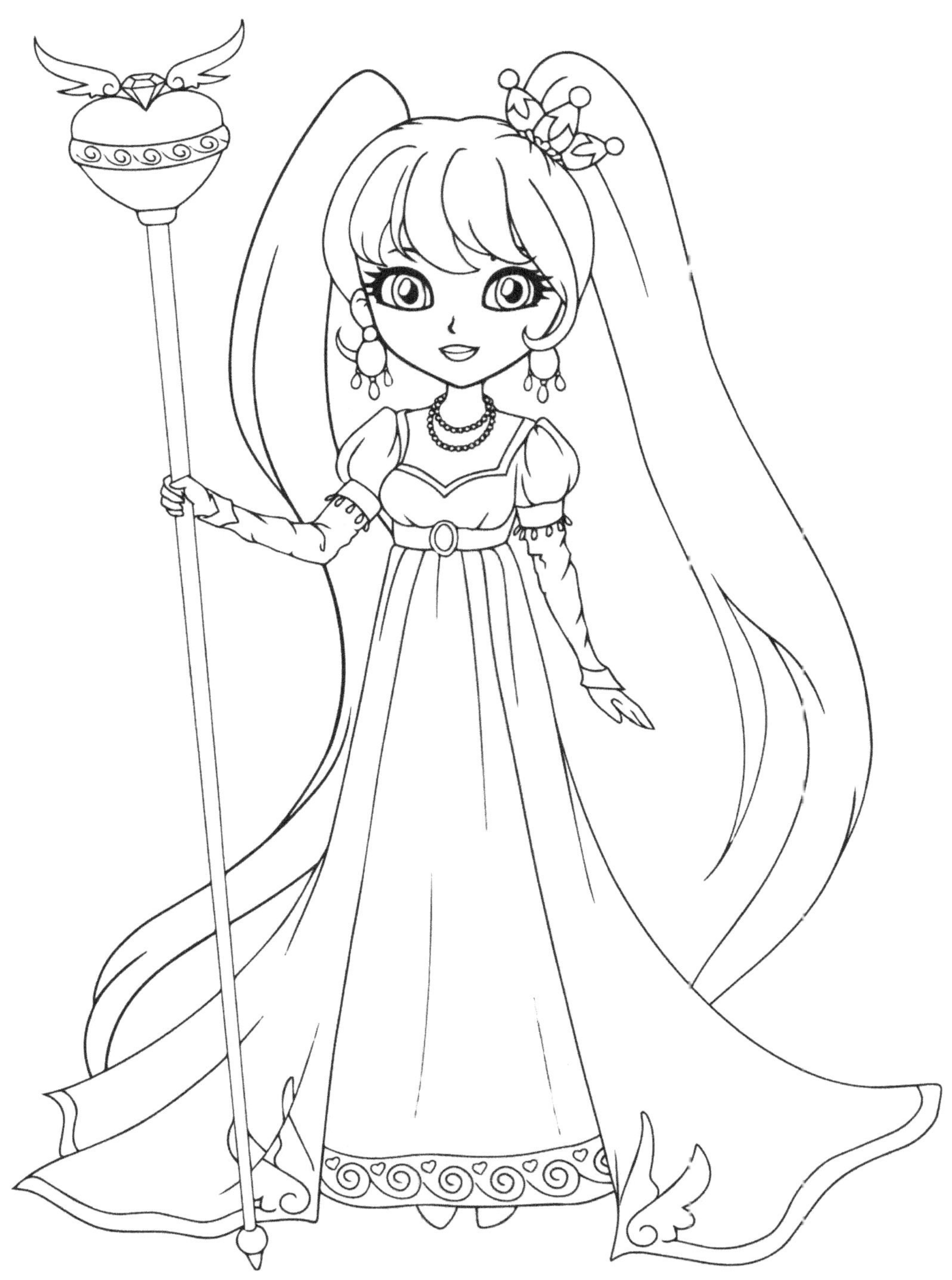

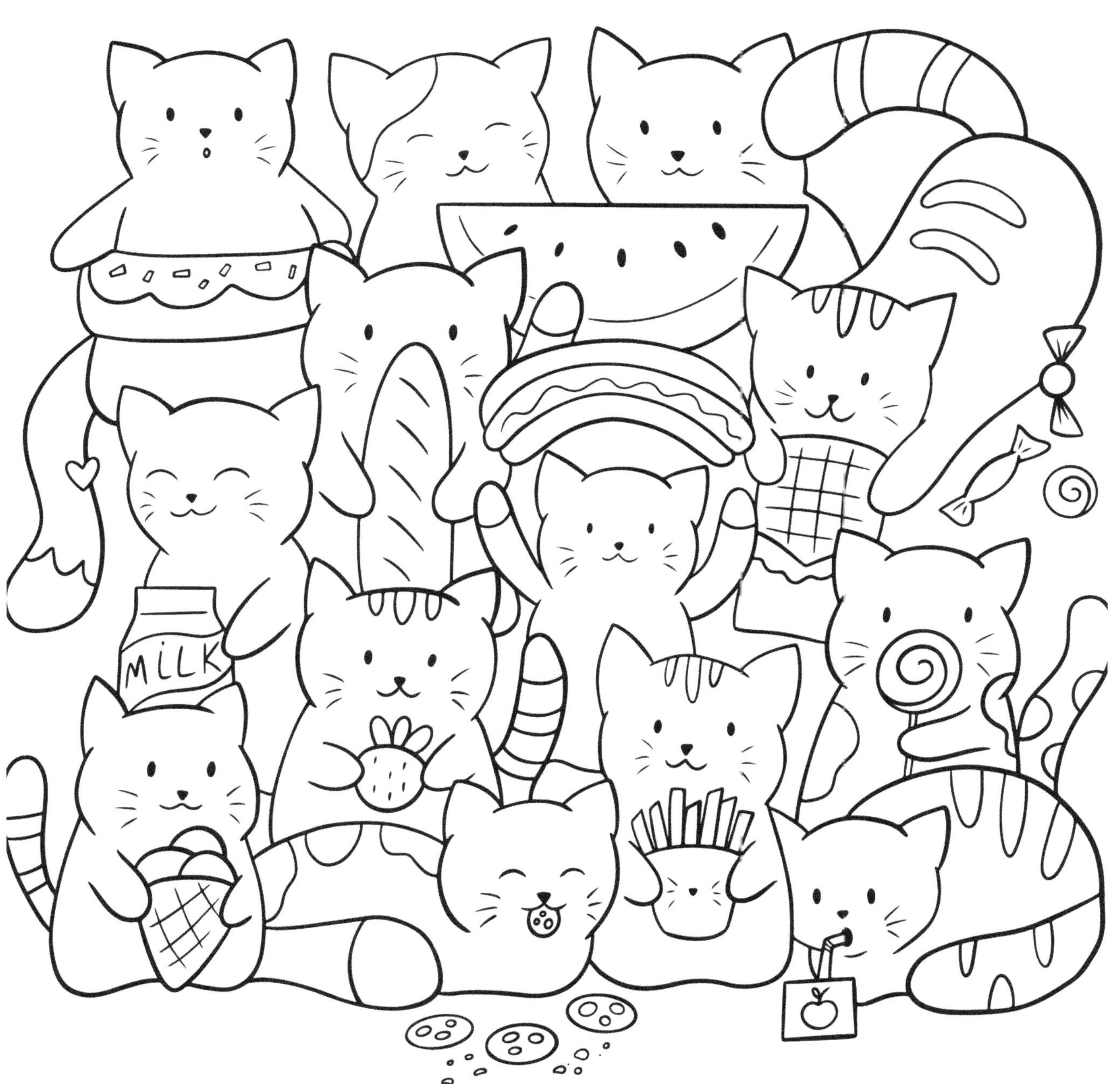

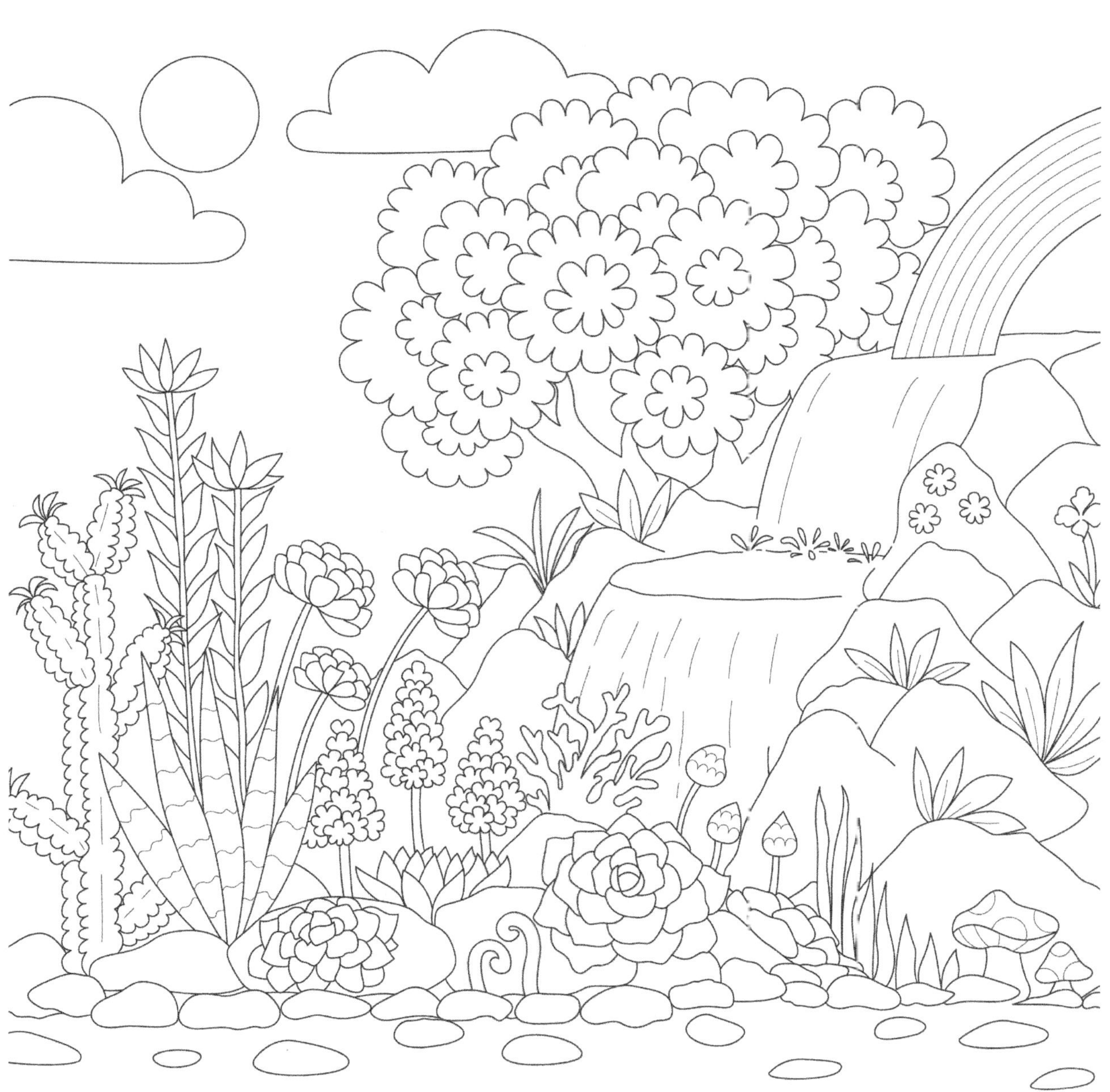

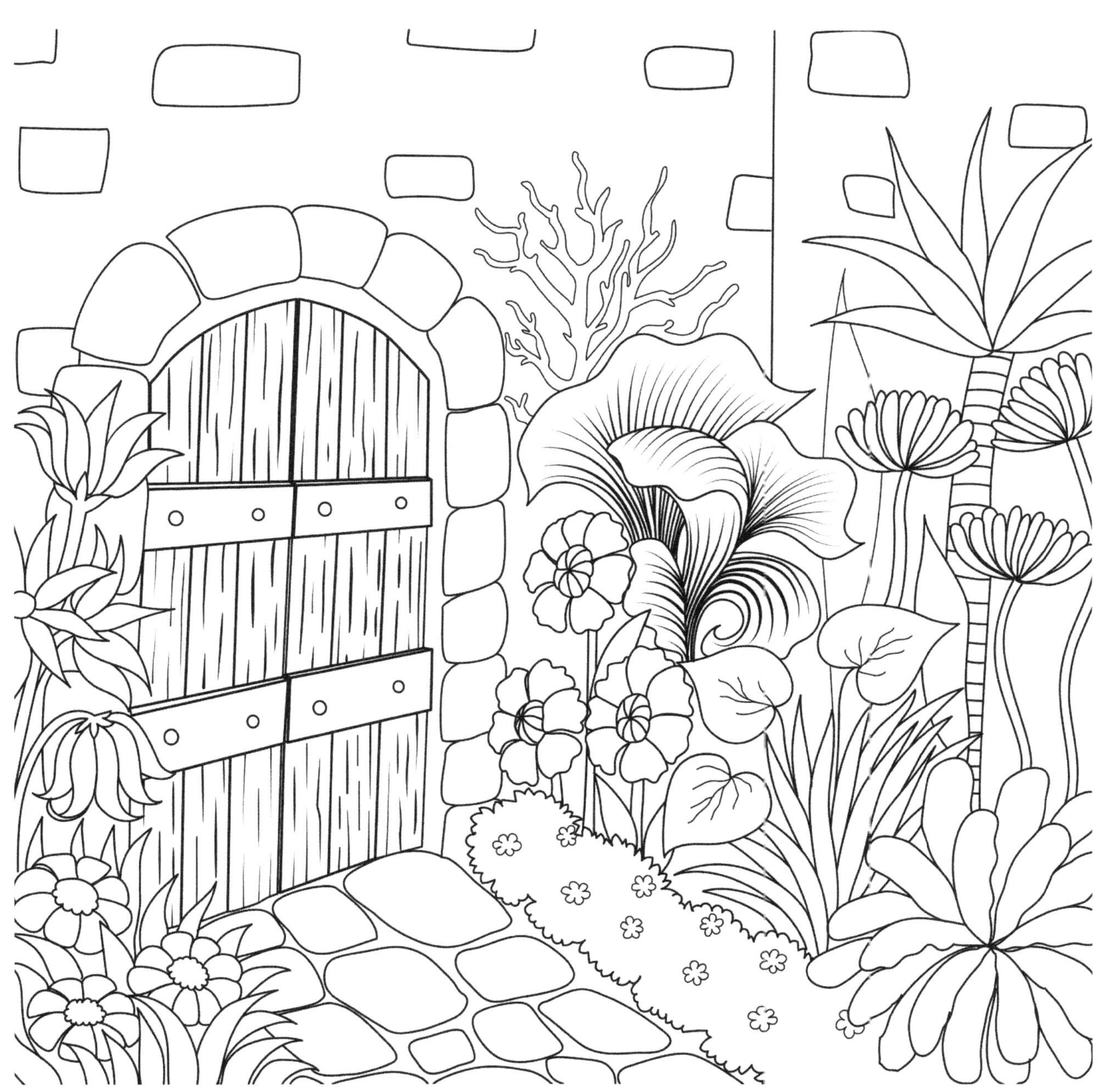

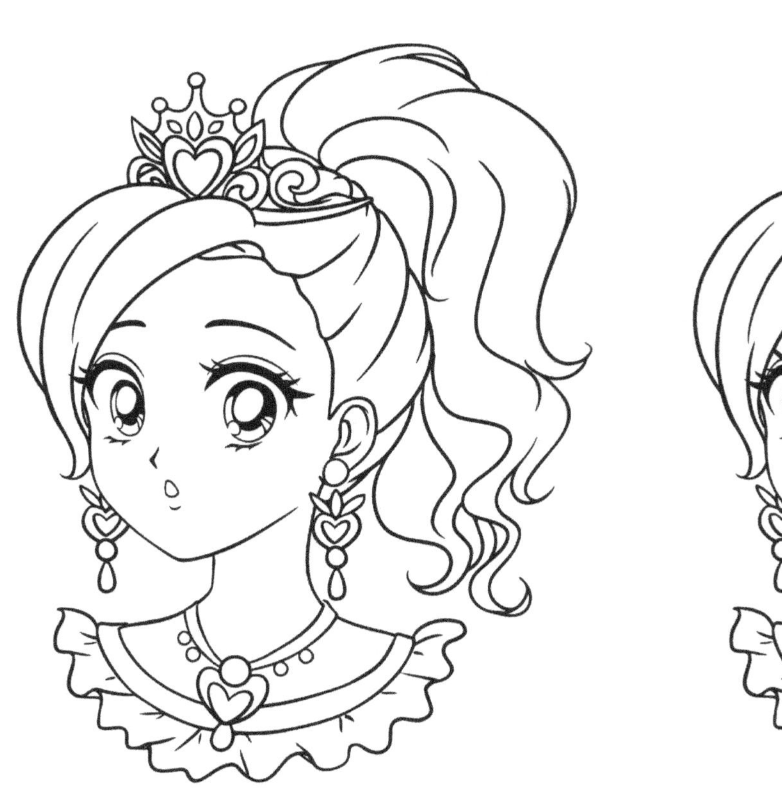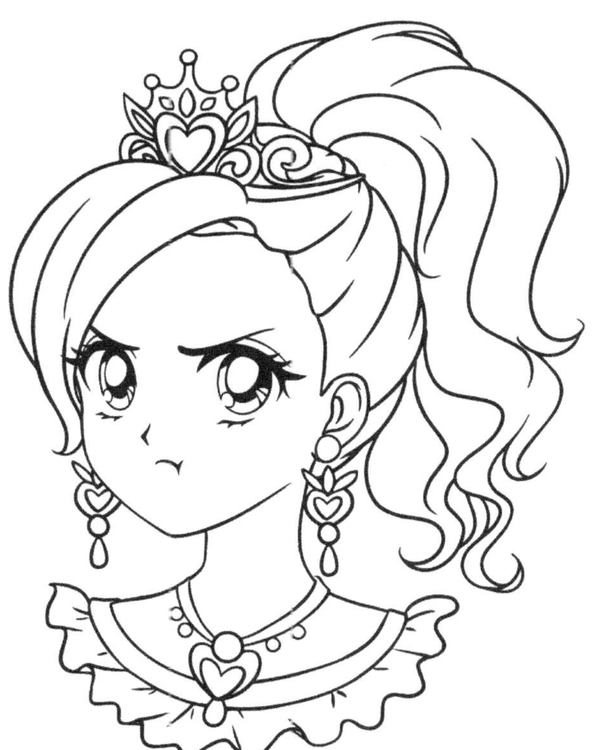

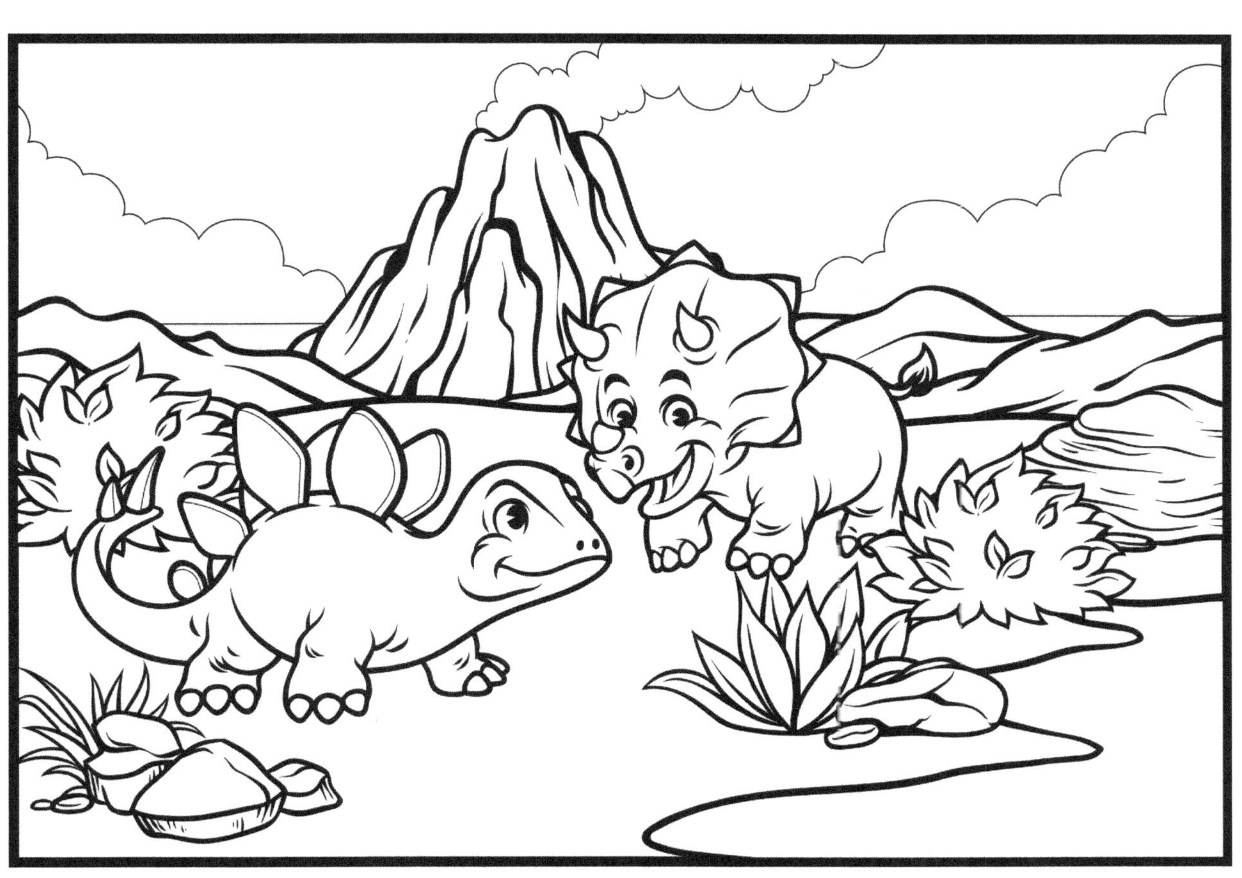

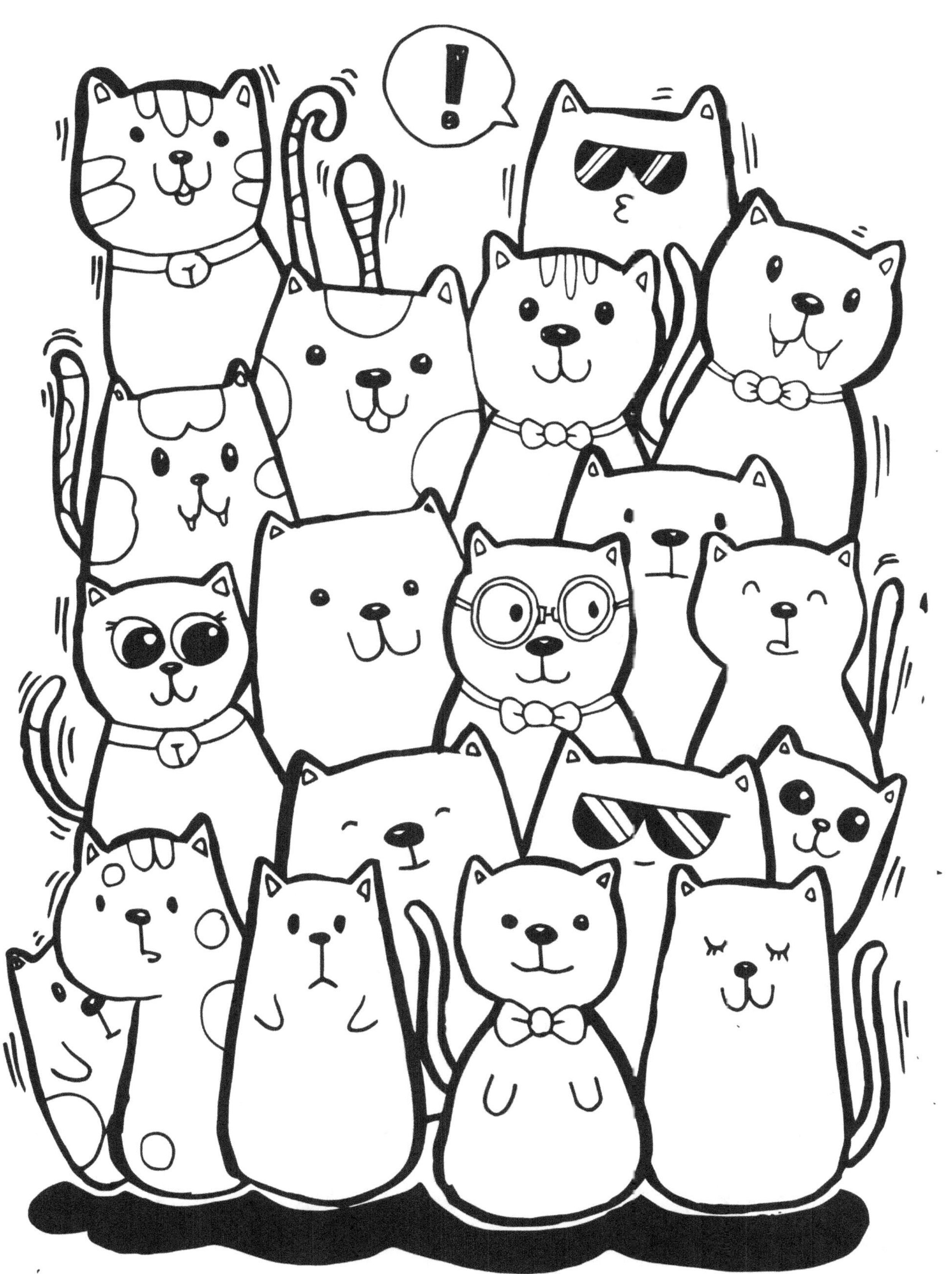

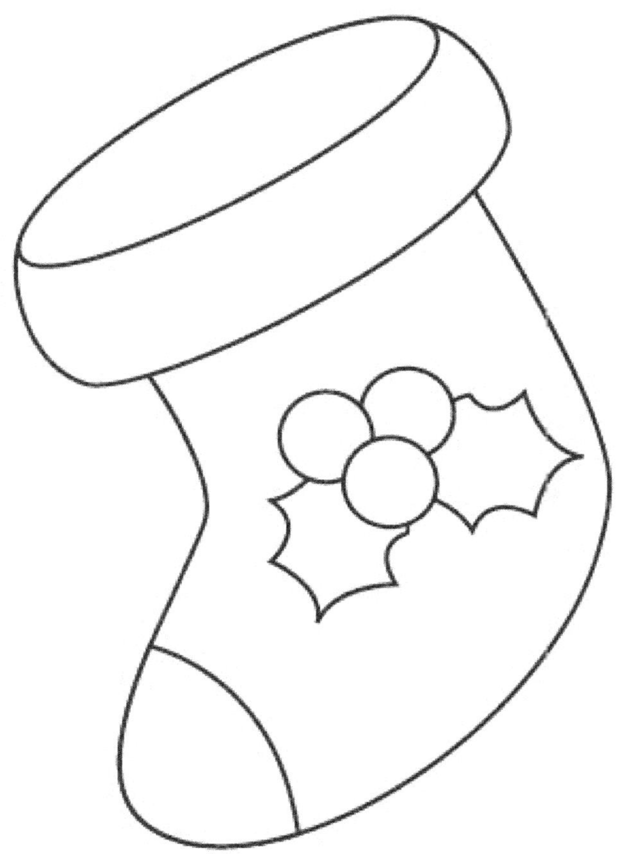

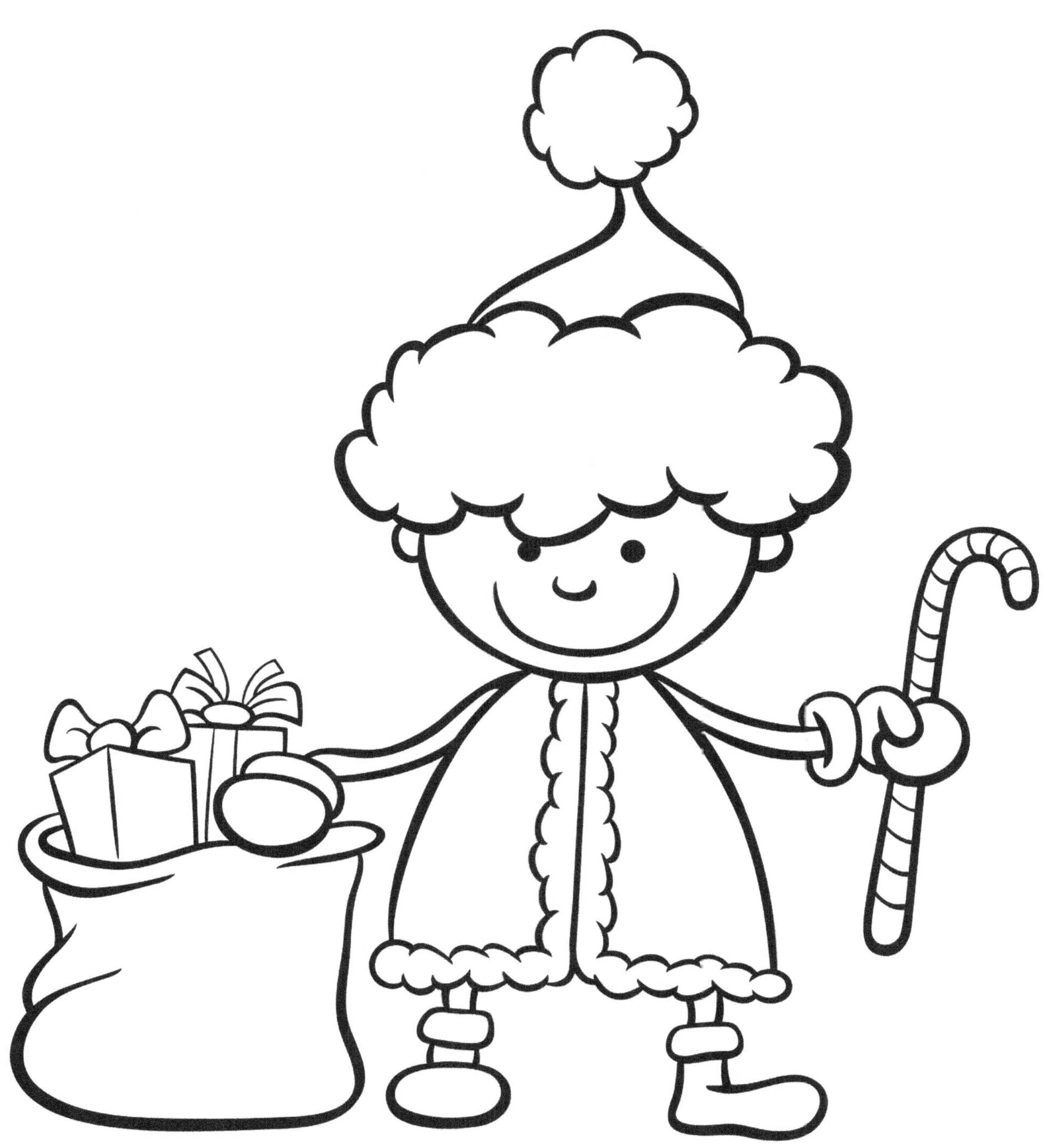

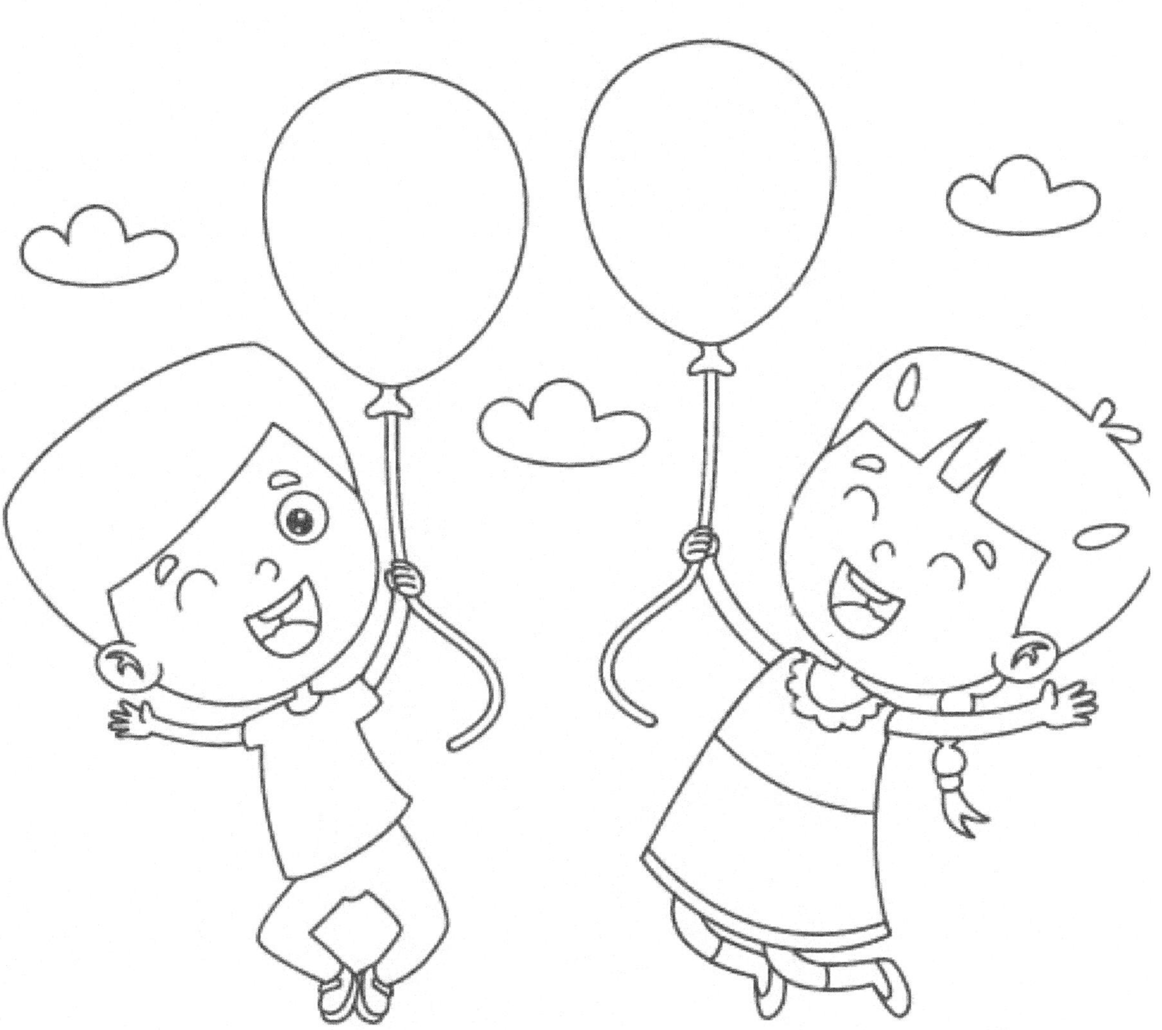

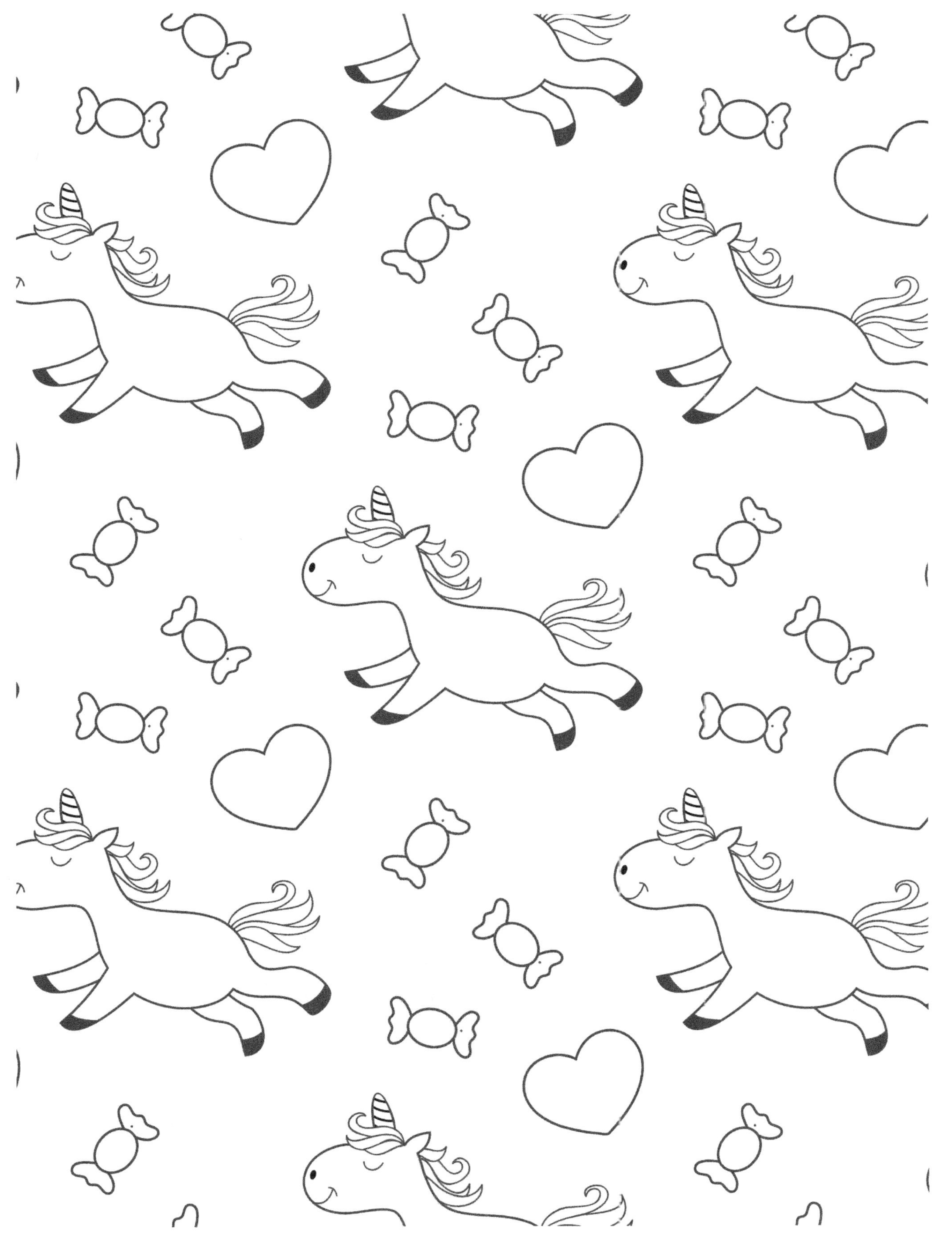

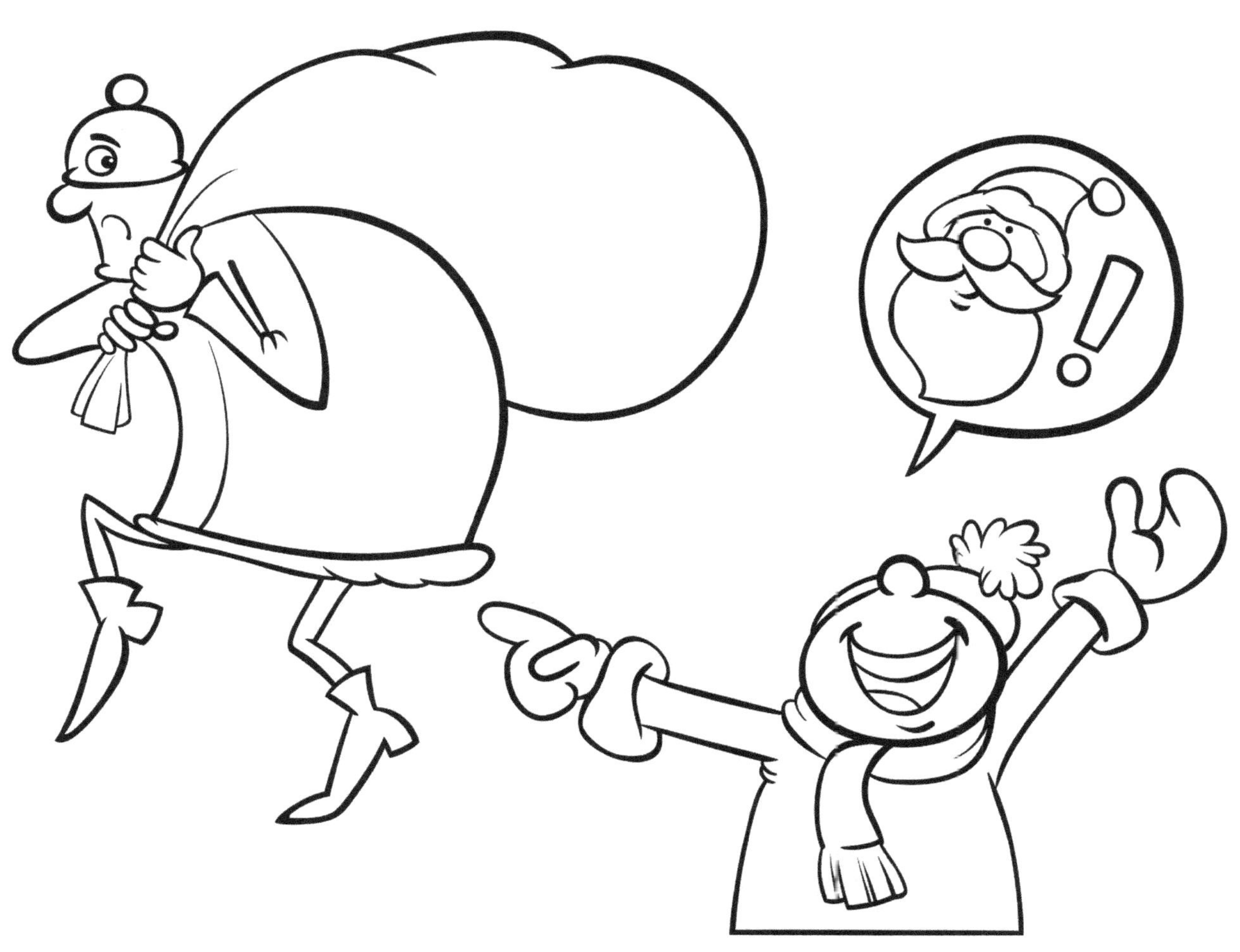

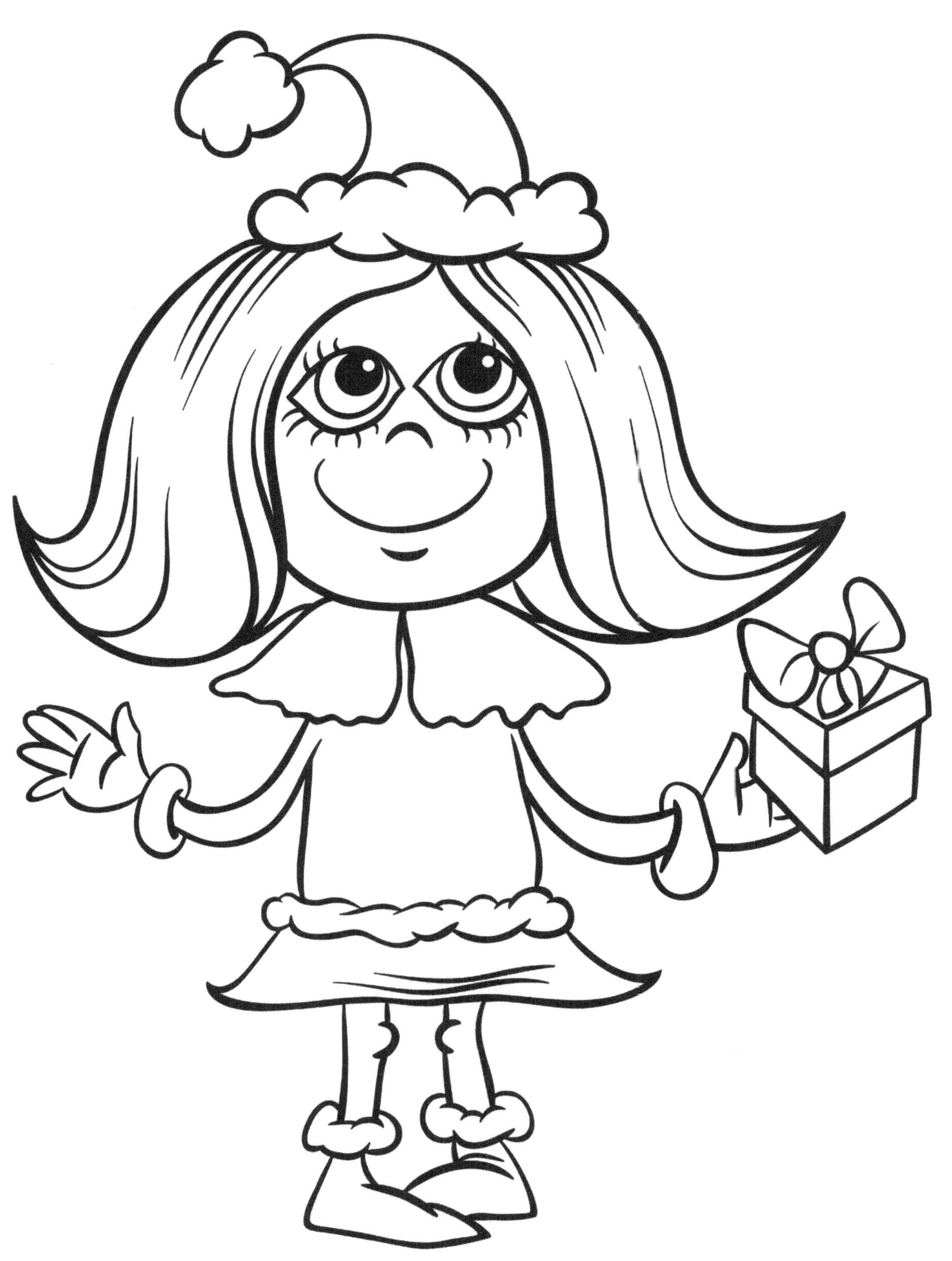

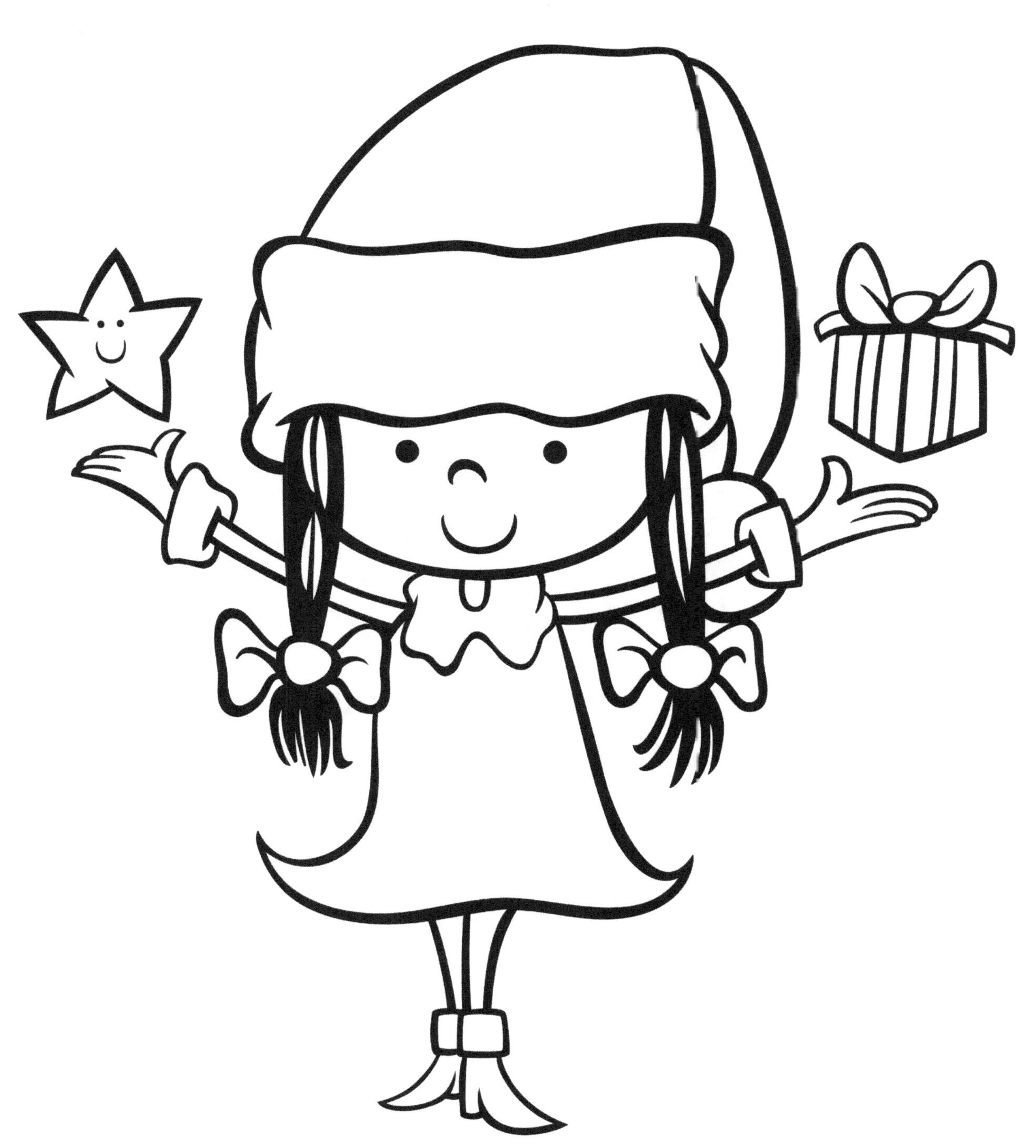

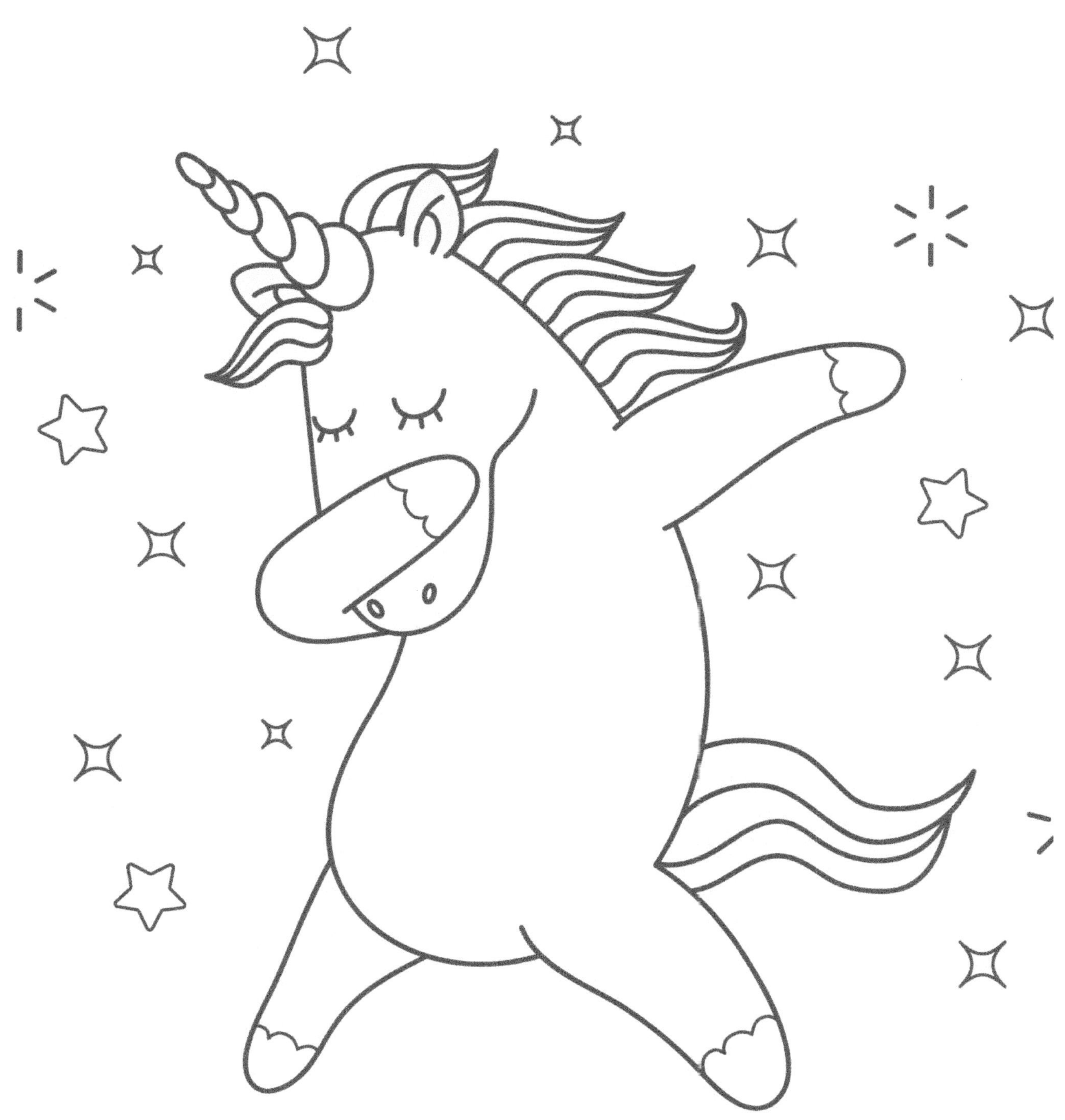

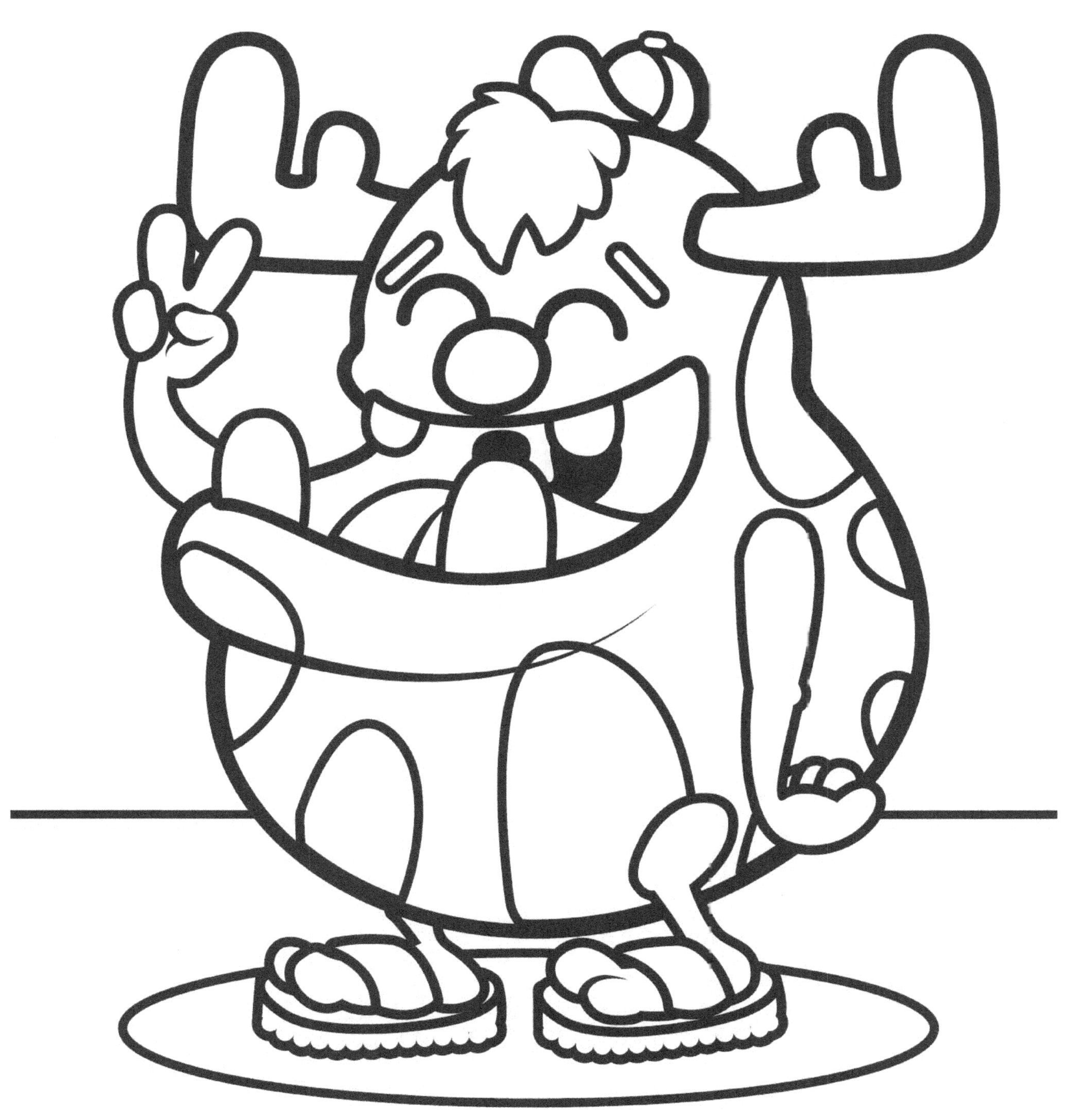

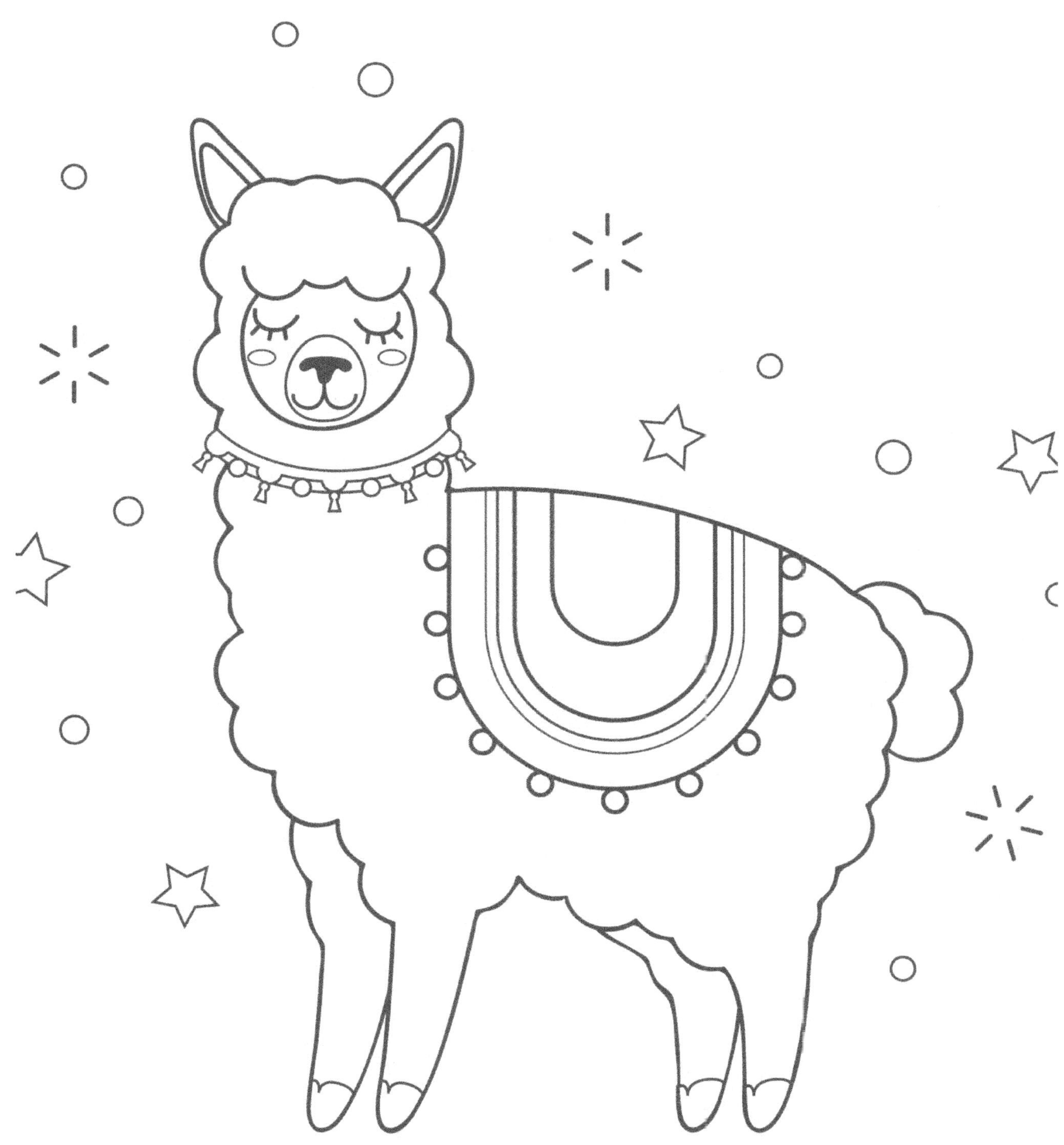

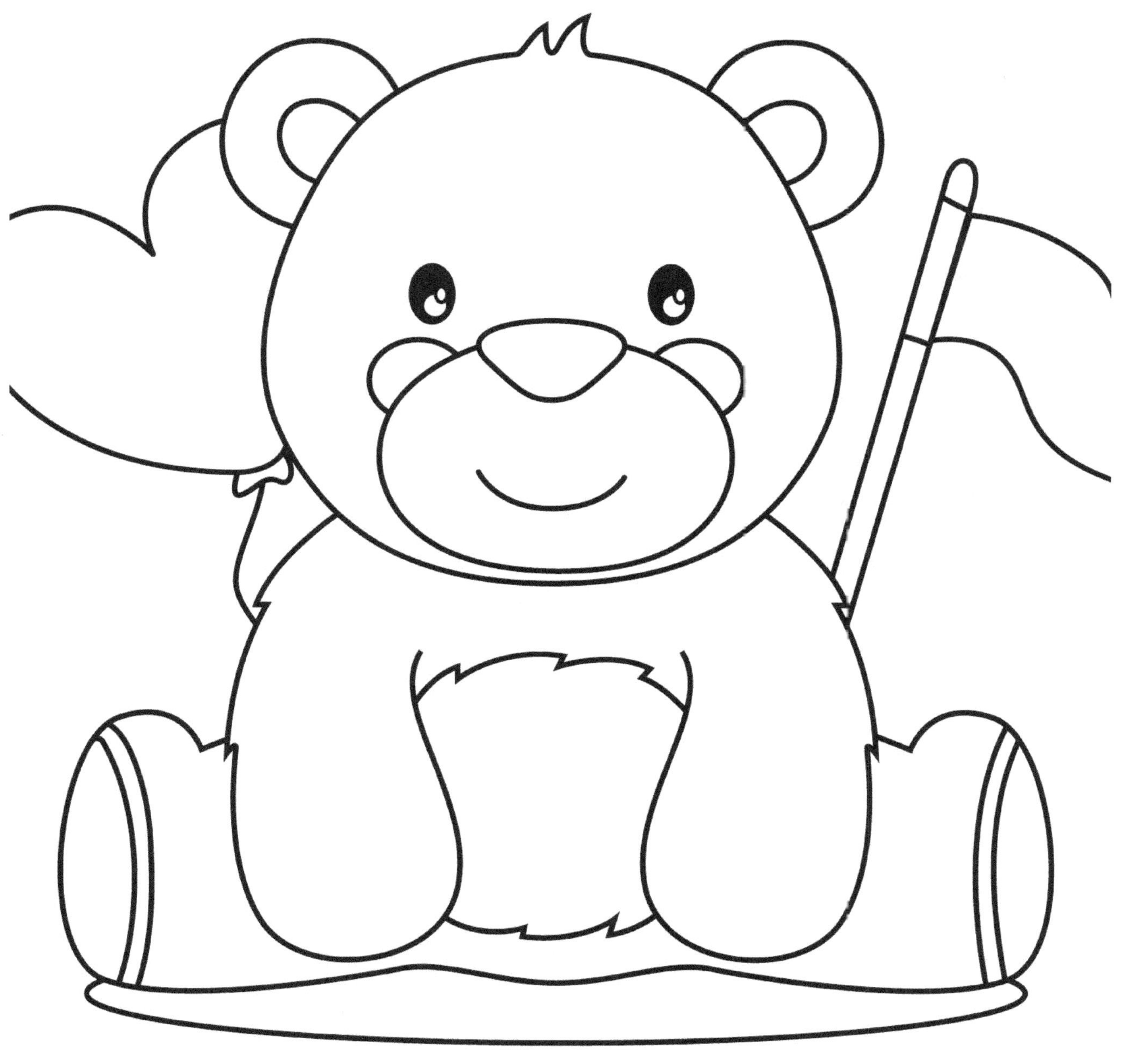

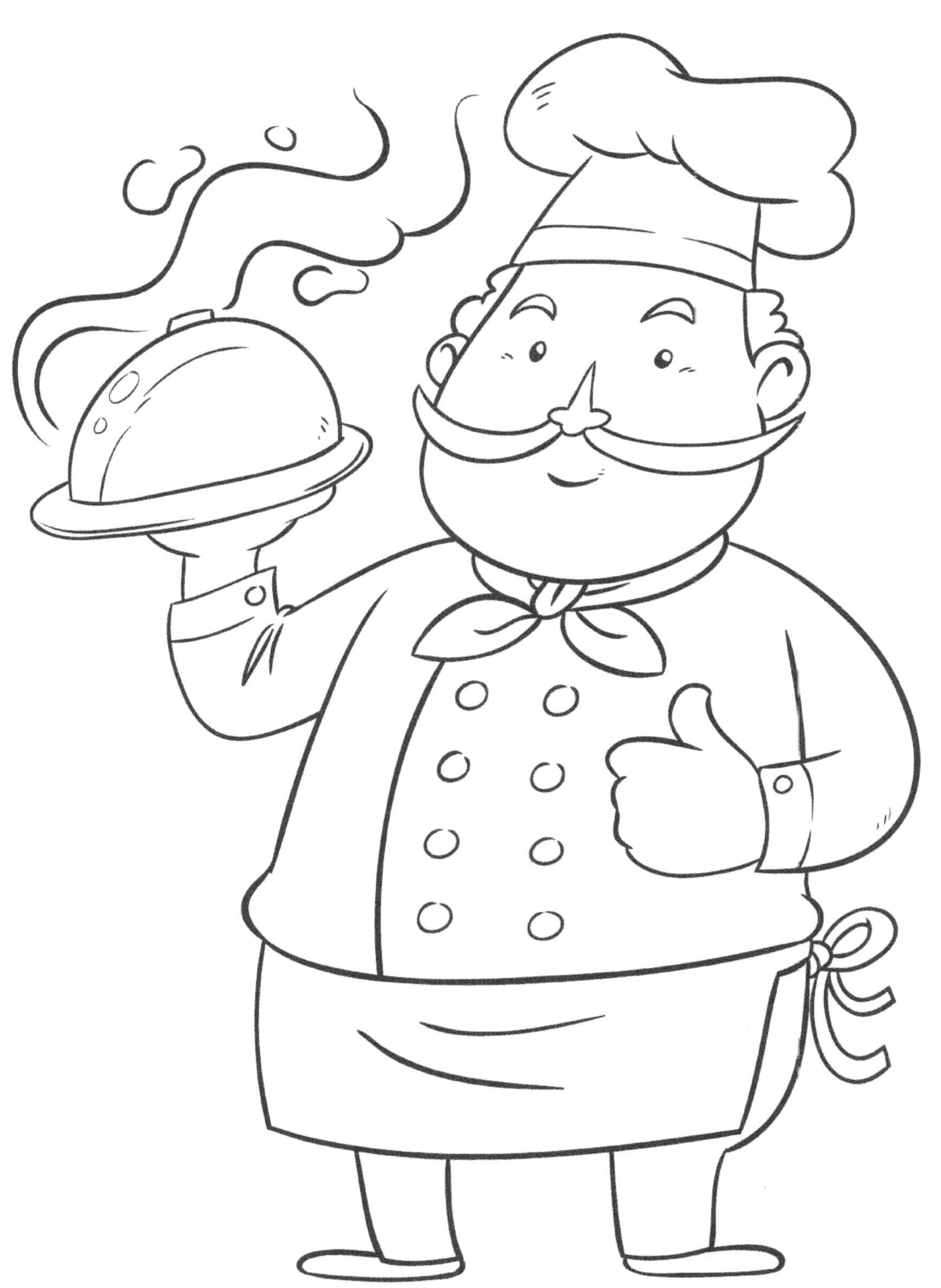

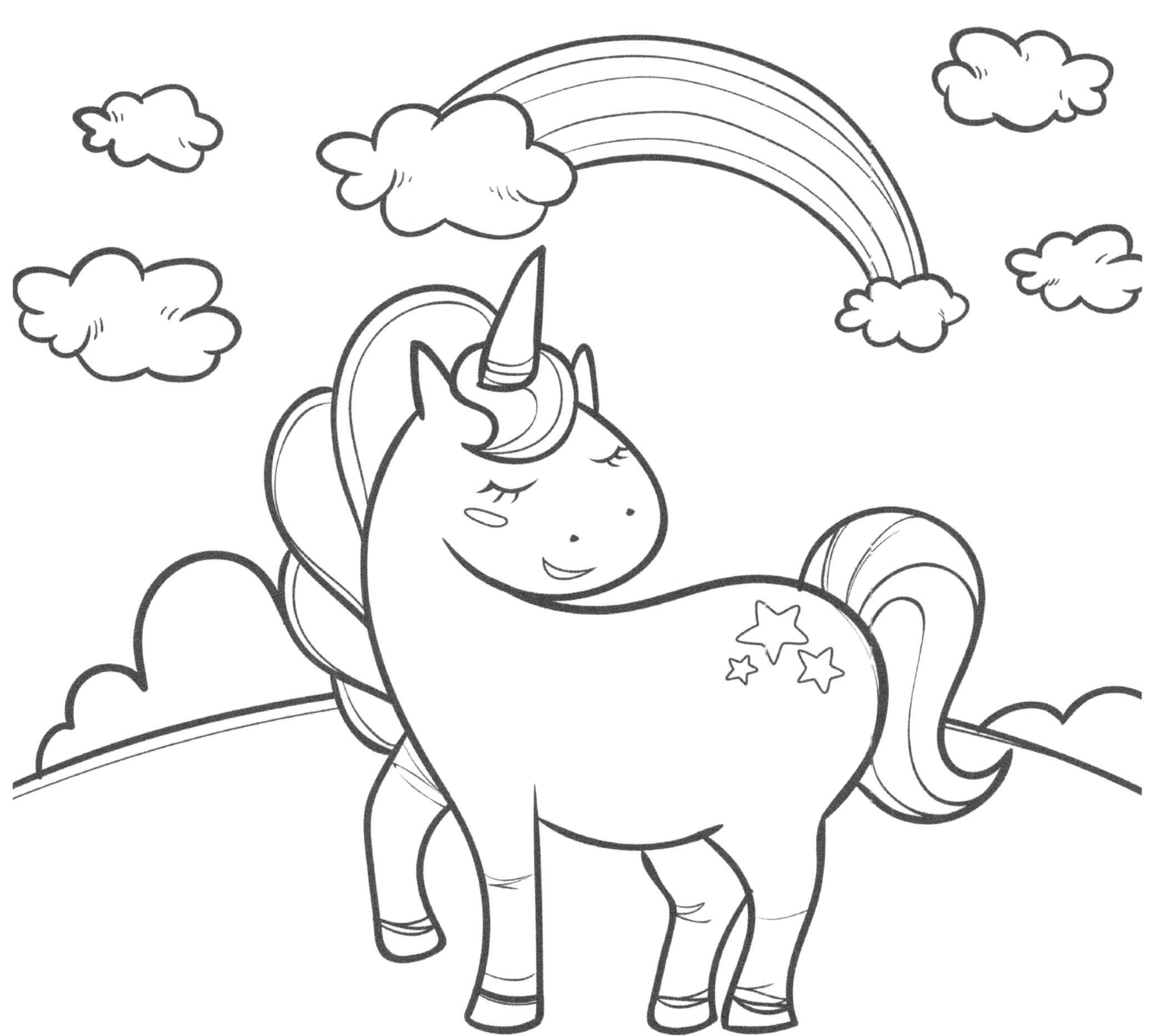

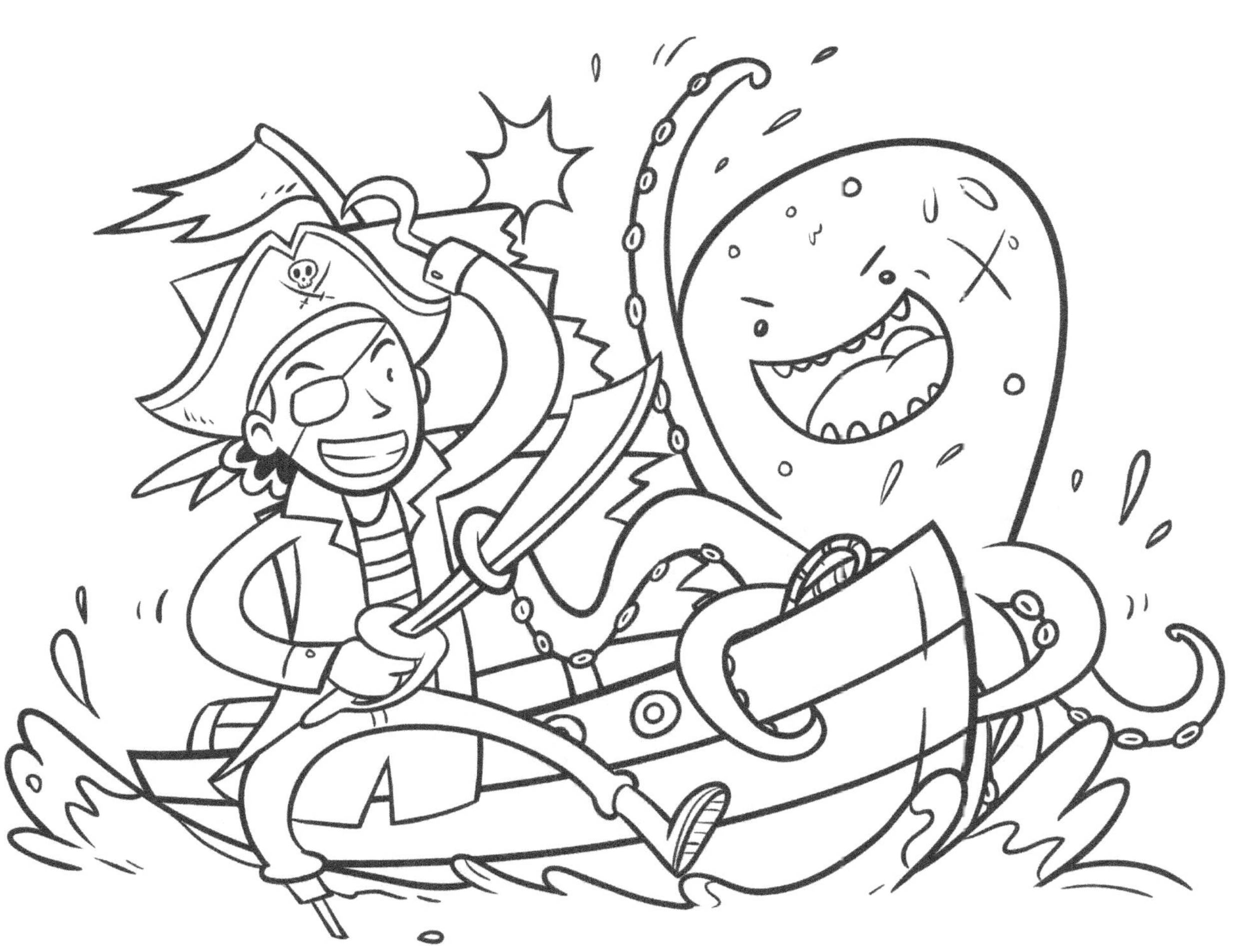

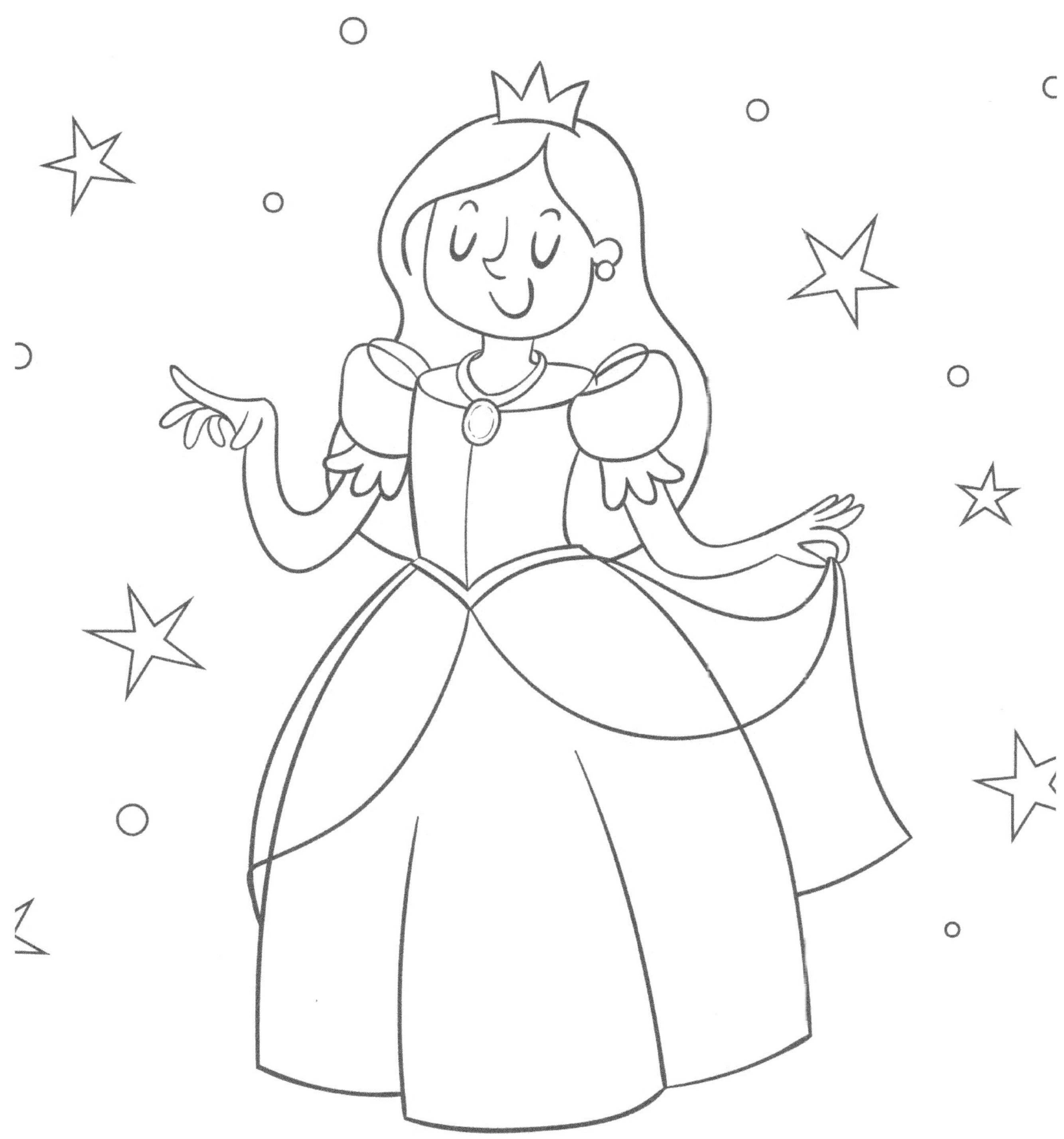

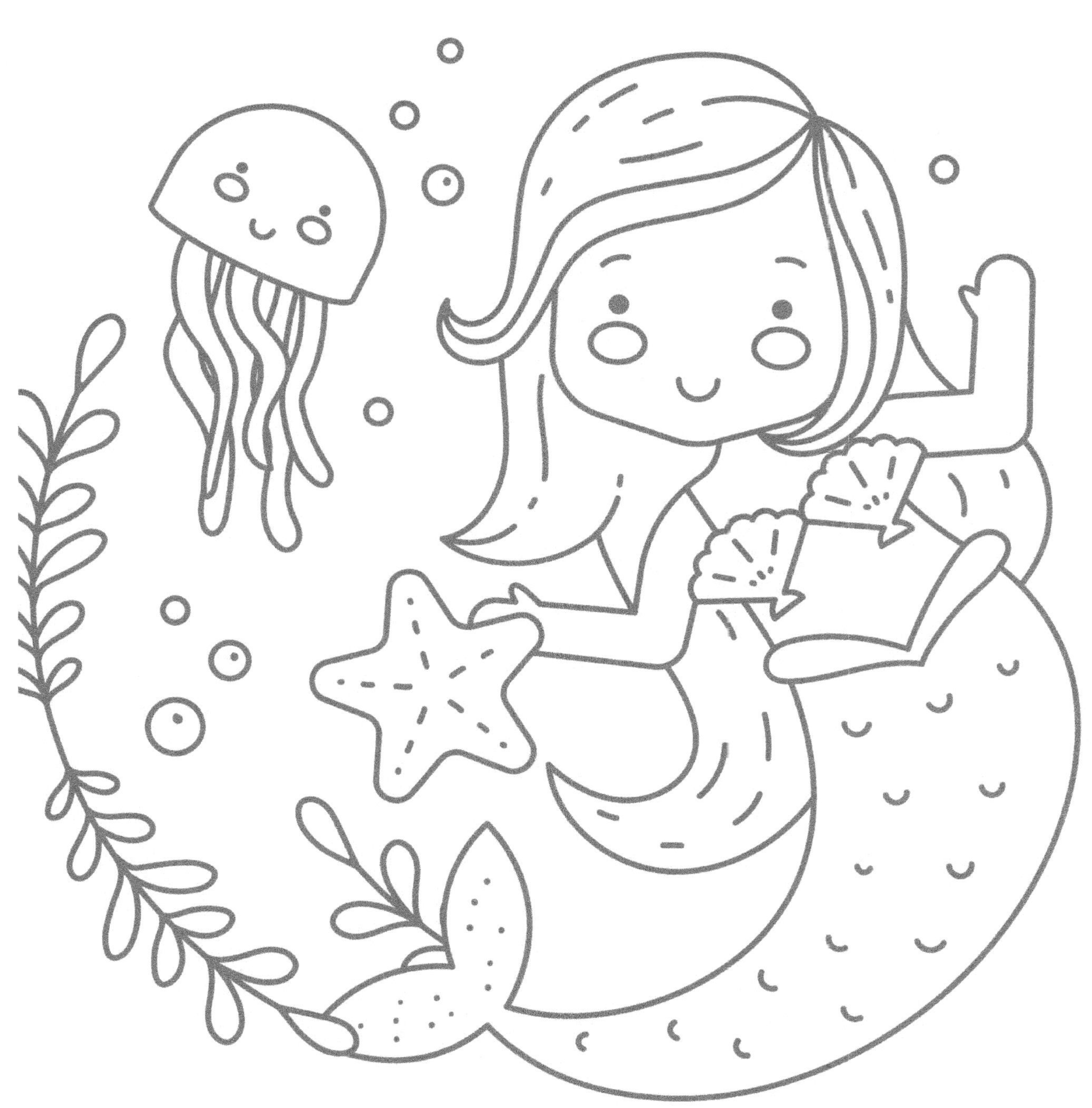

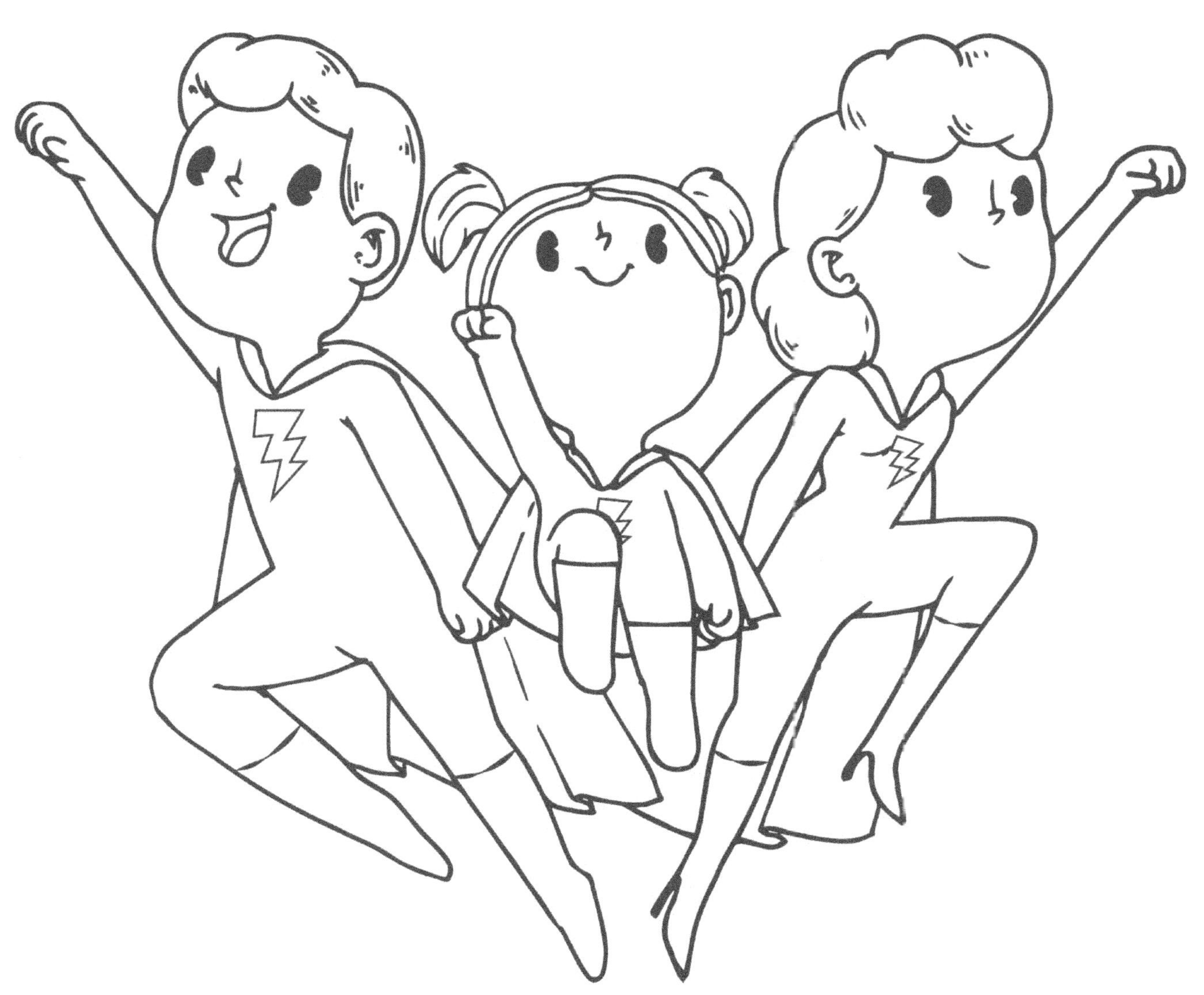

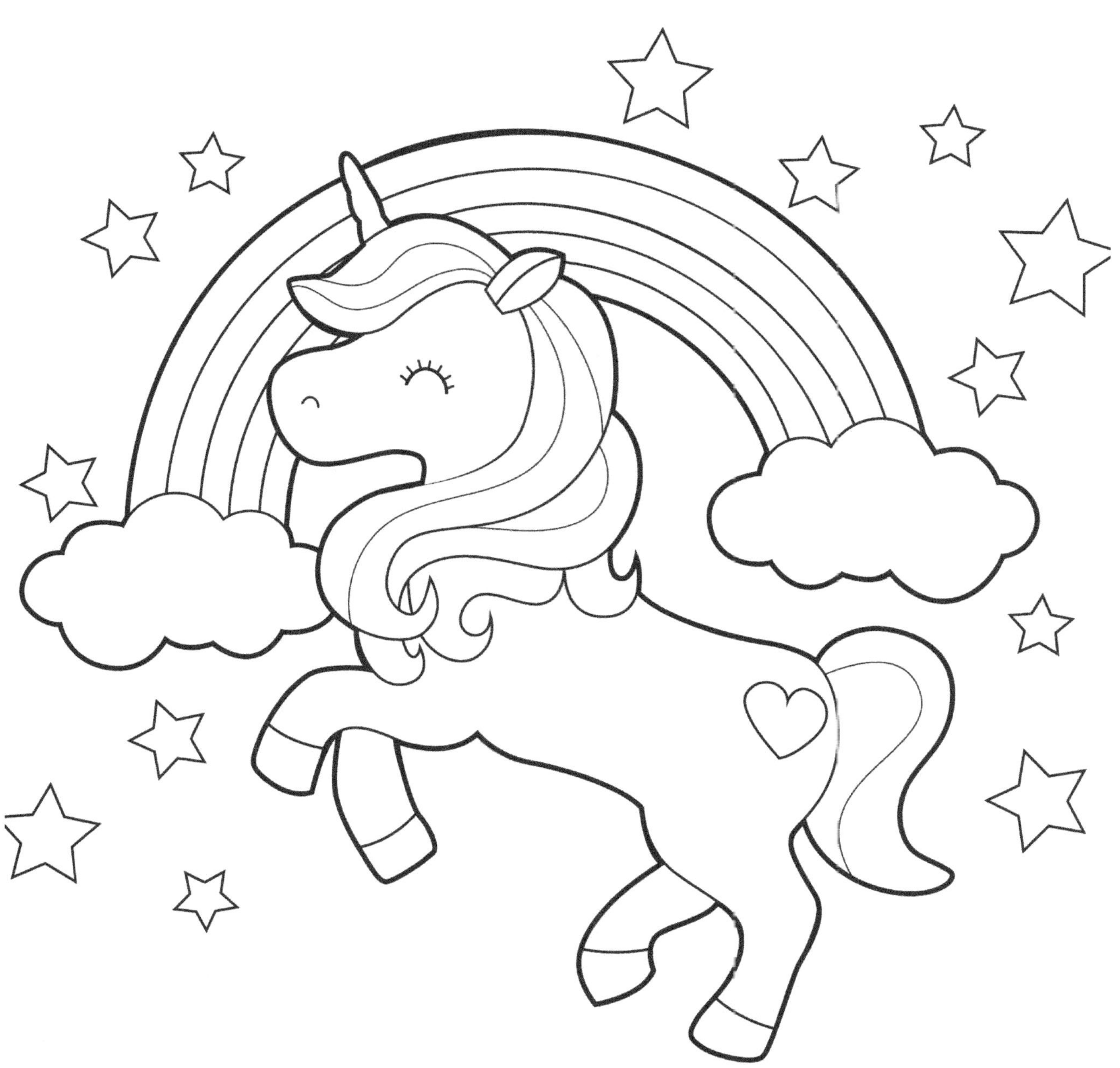

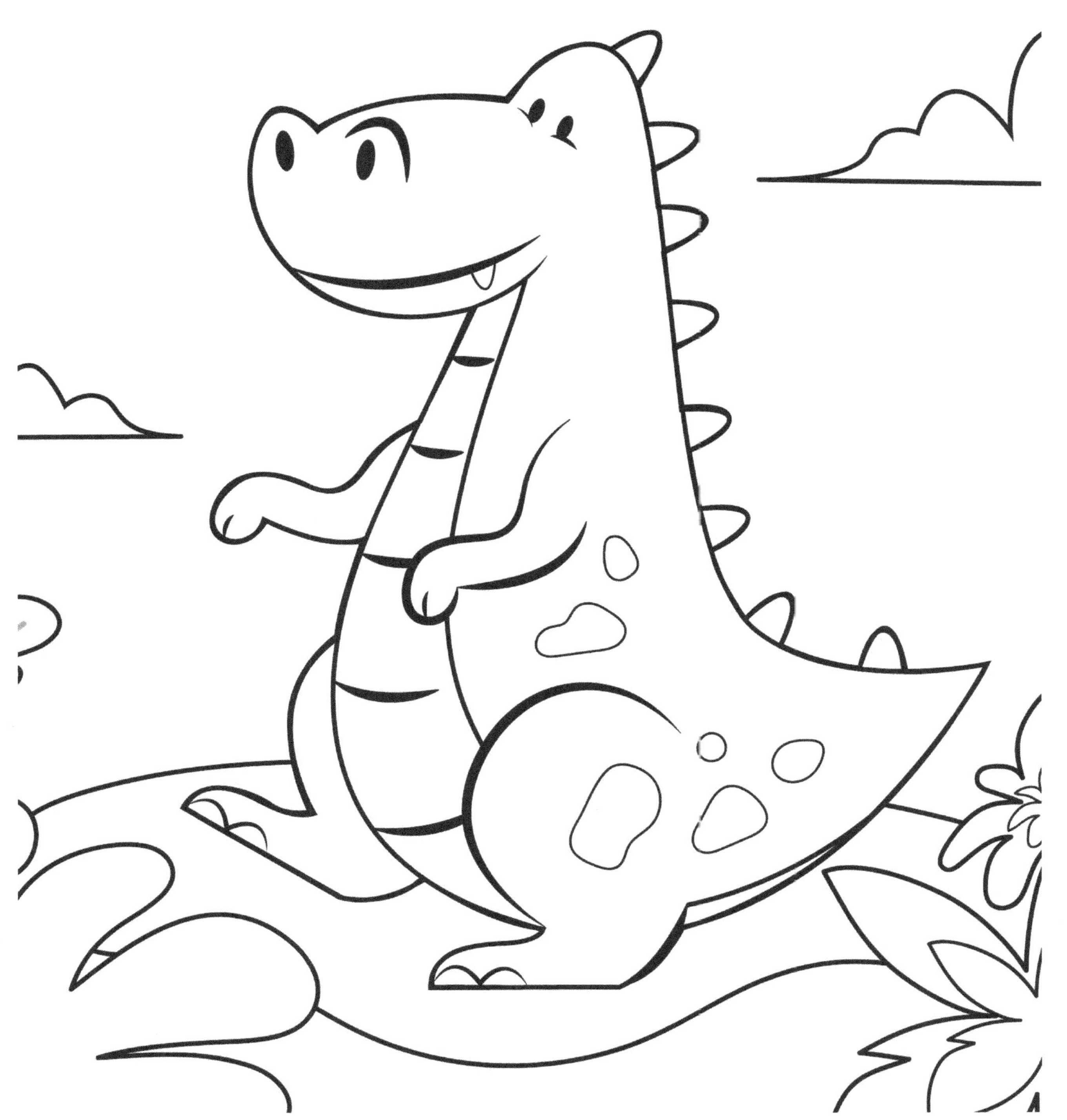

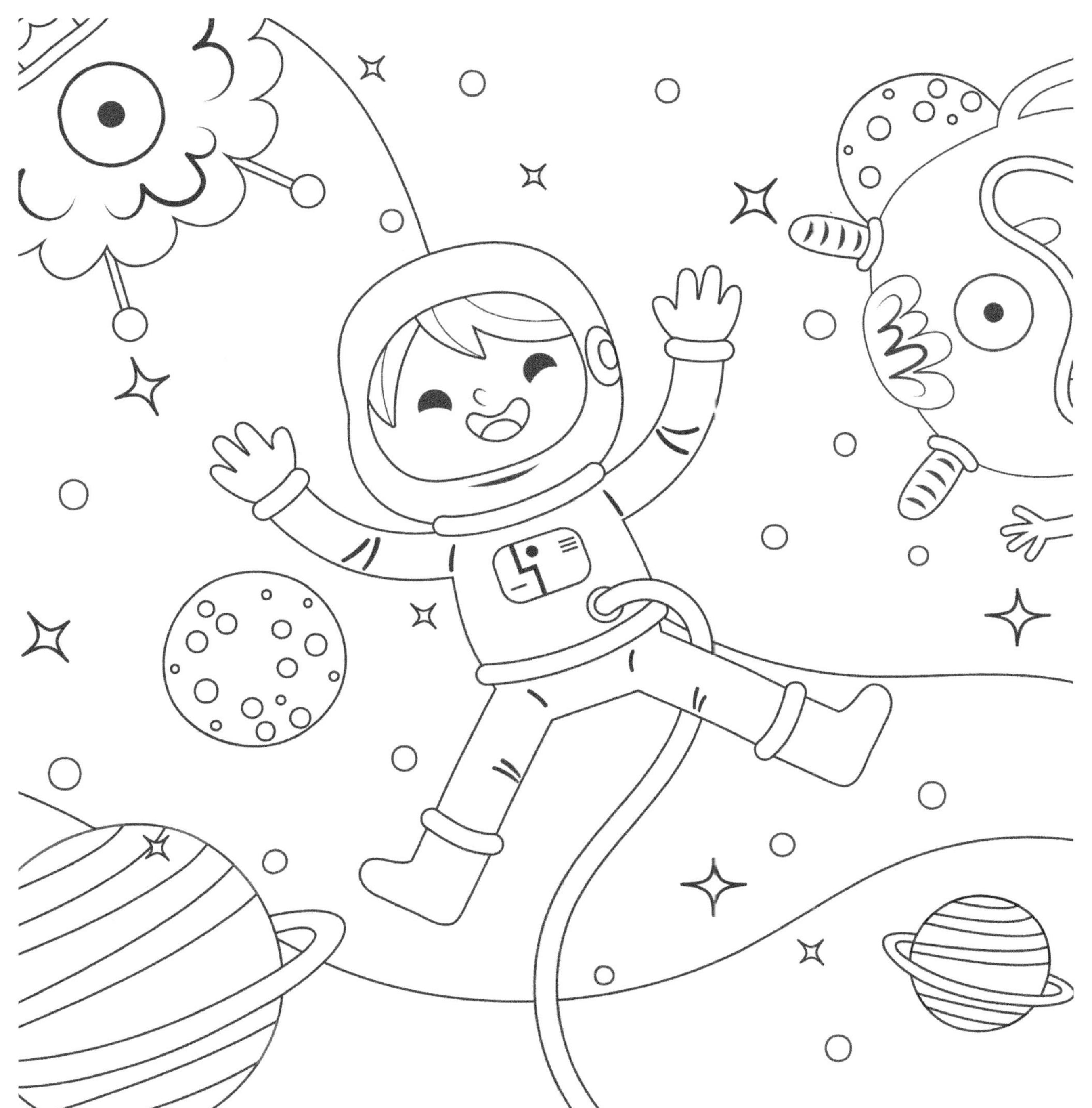

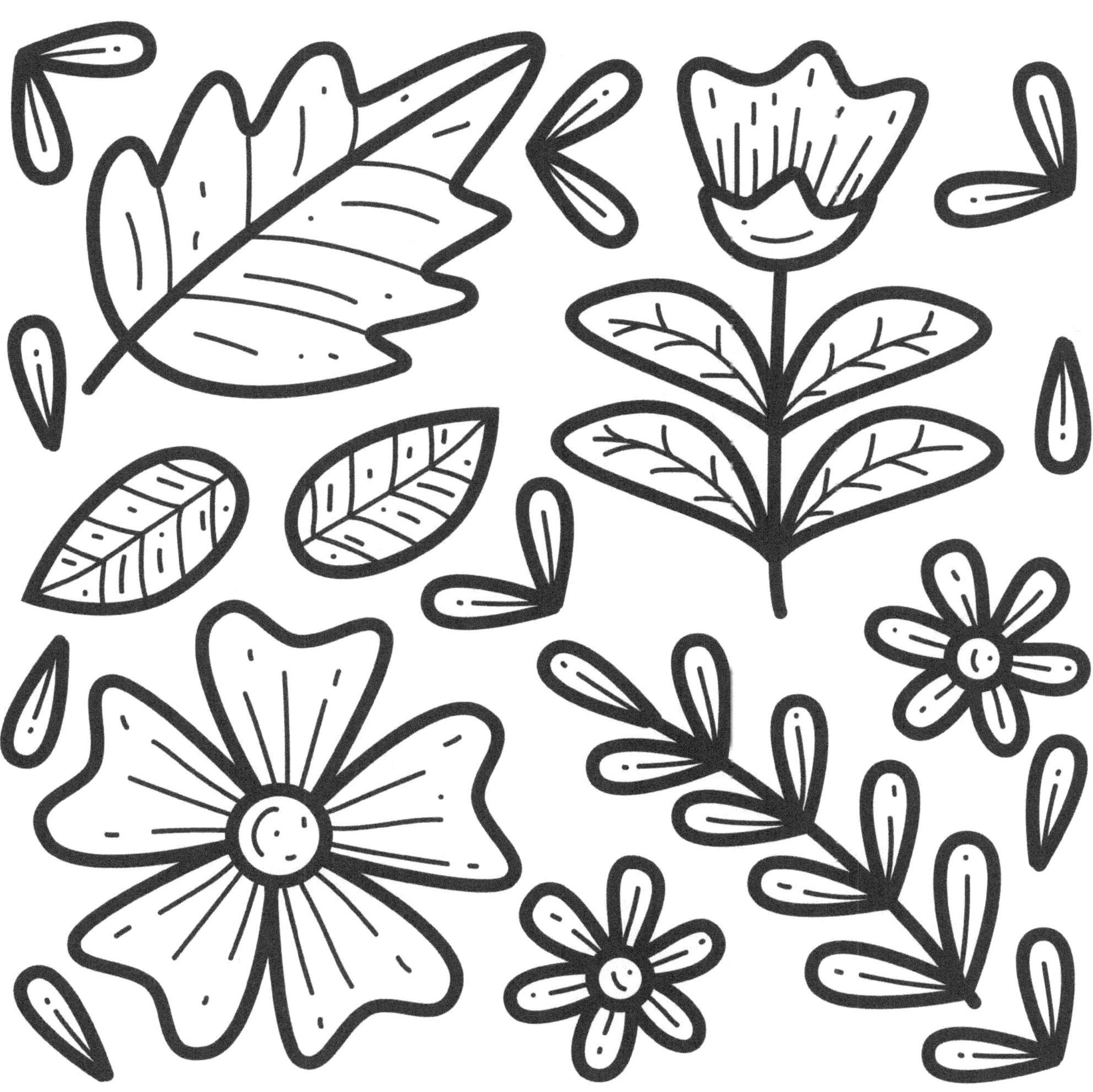

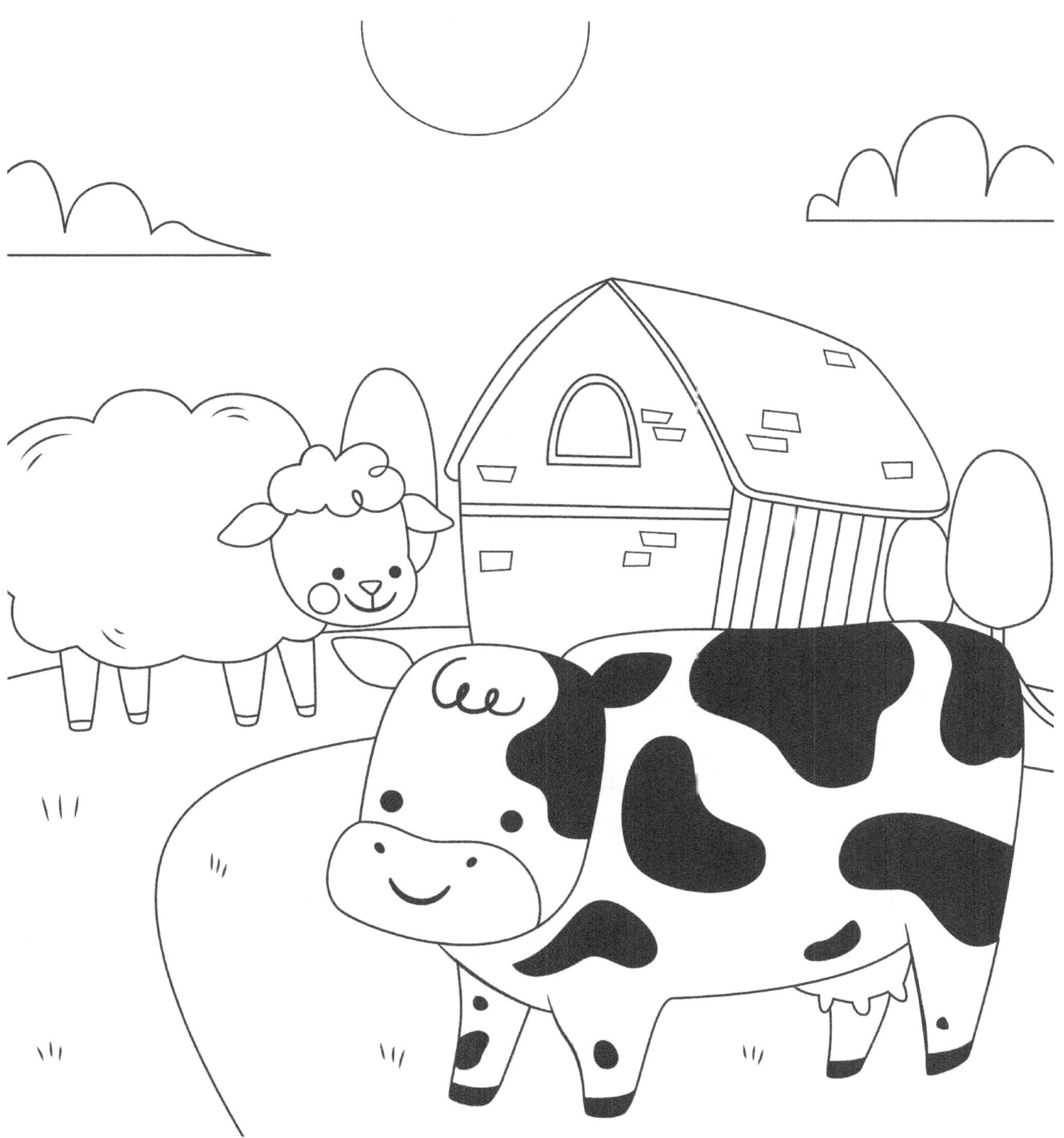

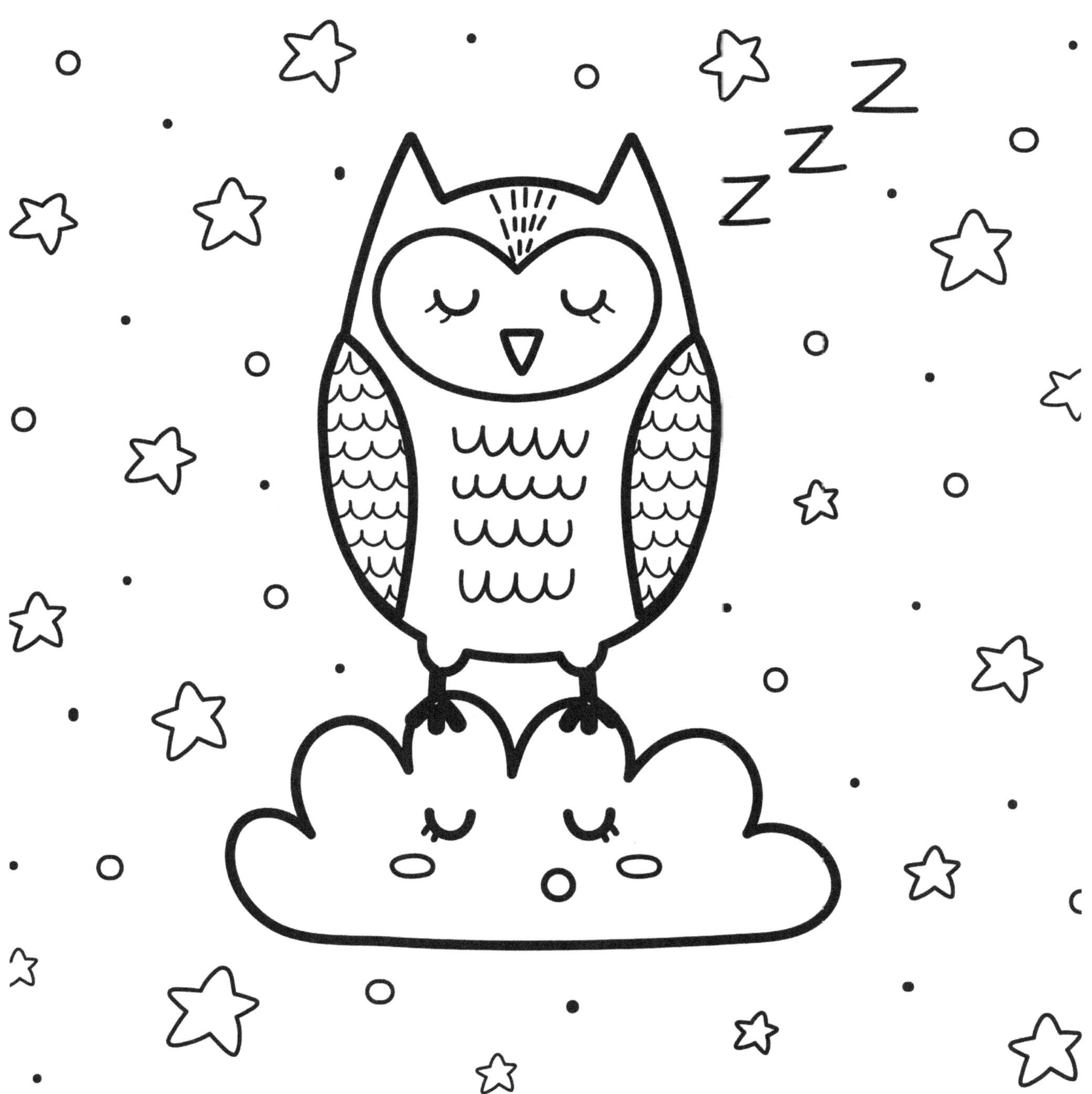

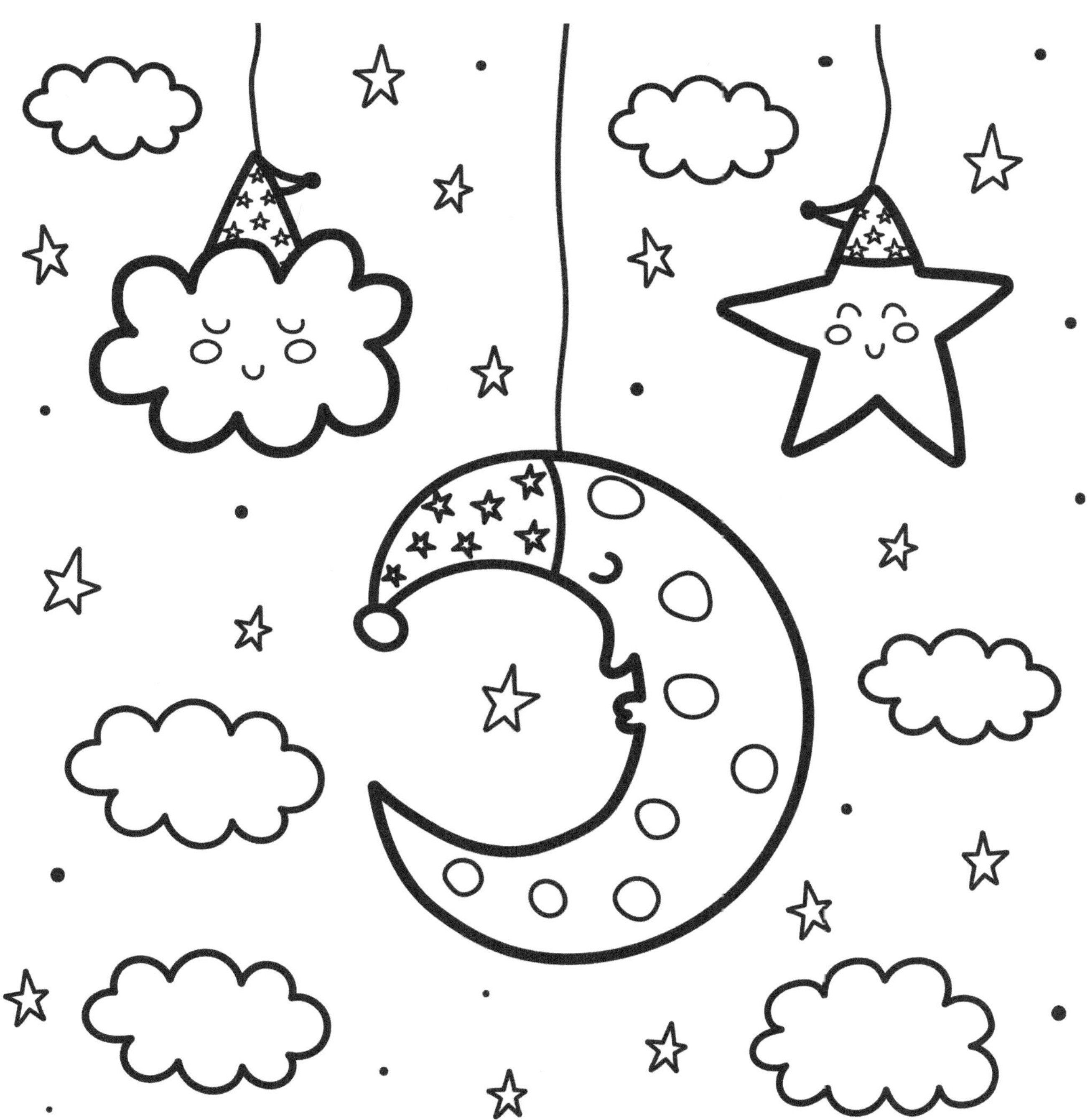

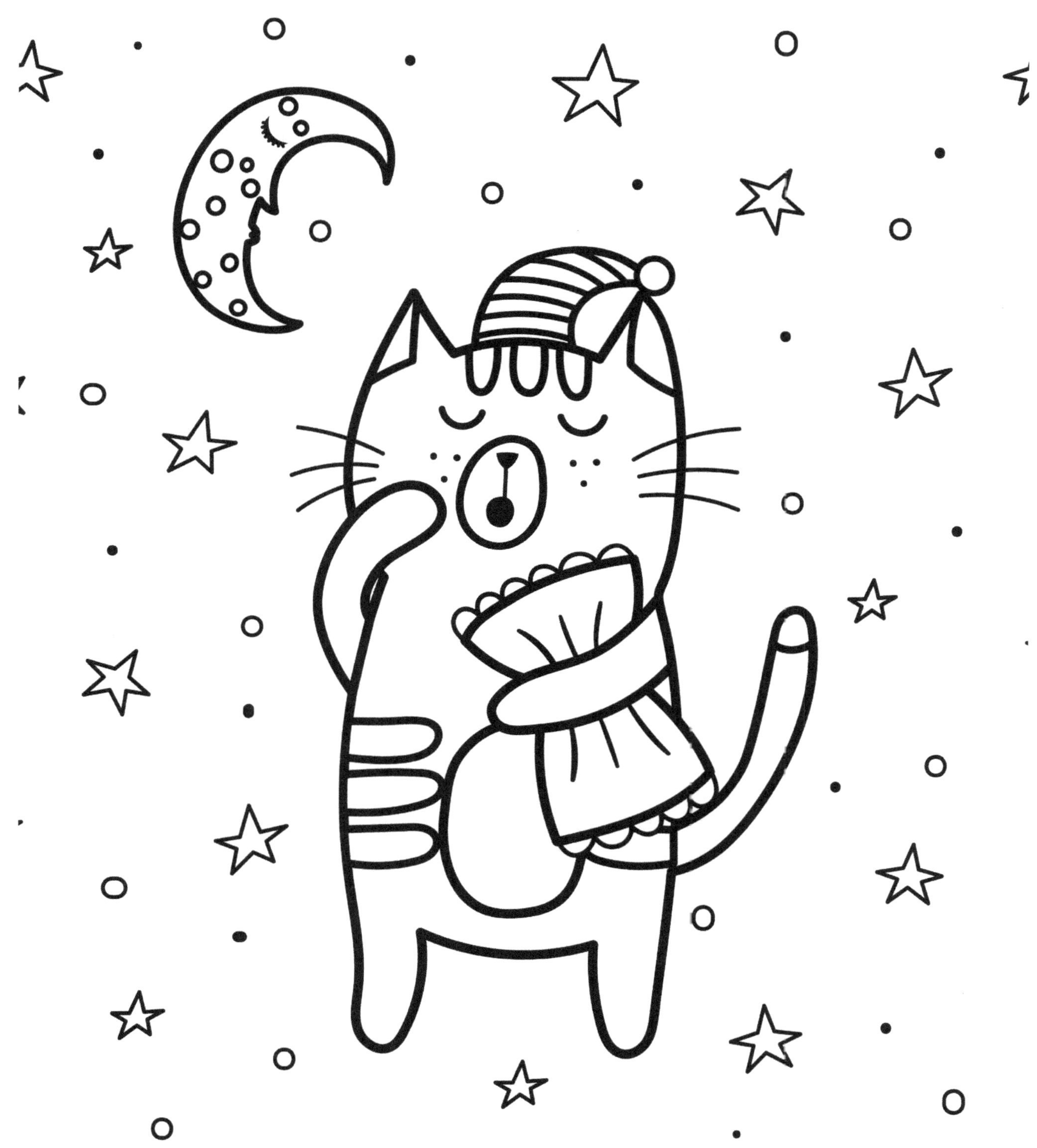

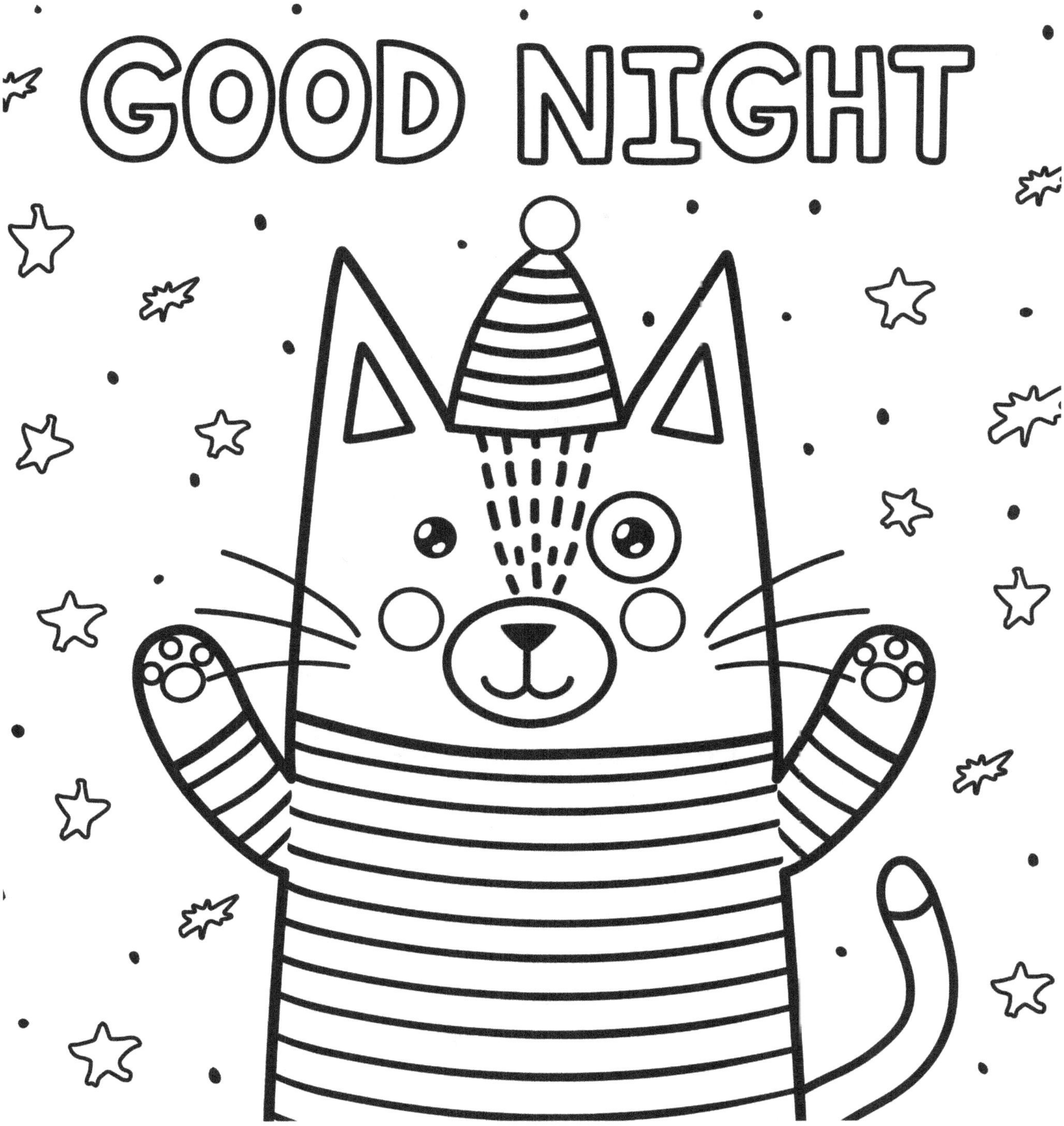

GOOD NIGHT

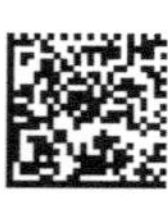
www.ingramcontent.com/pod-product-compliance
Lightning Source LLC
Chambersburg PA
CBHW081427250726
48654CB00013B/1838
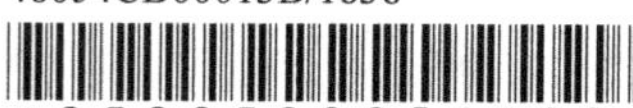